MUMBAI METRO TRANSFORMING TRANSPORT
CONTRIBUTING TOWARD AN EQUITABLE, SAFER, AND CLEANER CITY

JUNE 2021

ASIAN DEVELOPMENT BANK

 Creative Commons Attribution 3.0 IGO license (CC BY 3.0 IGO)

© 2021 Asian Development Bank
6 ADB Avenue, Mandaluyong City, 1550 Metro Manila, Philippines
Tel +63 2 8632 4444; Fax +63 2 8636 2444
www.adb.org

Some rights reserved. Published in 2021.

ISBN 978-92-9262-849-9 (print); 978-92-9262-850-5 (electronic); 978-92-9262-851-2 (ebook)
Publication Stock No. SPR210179
DOI: http://dx.doi.org/10.22617/SPR210179

The views expressed in this publication are those of the authors and do not necessarily reflect the views and policies of the Asian Development Bank (ADB) or its Board of Governors or the governments they represent. The study reflects the views of the authors and does not necessarily reflect the views of either the Government of India or ADB. The findings of the study are not binding on either the Government of India or ADB.

ADB does not guarantee the accuracy of the data included in this publication and accepts no responsibility for any consequence of their use. The mention of specific companies or products of manufacturers does not imply that they are endorsed or recommended by ADB in preference to others of a similar nature that are not mentioned.

By making any designation of or reference to a particular territory or geographic area, or by using the term "country" in this document, ADB does not intend to make any judgments as to the legal or other status of any territory or area.

This work is available under the Creative Commons Attribution 3.0 IGO license (CC BY 3.0 IGO) https://creativecommons.org/licenses/by/3.0/igo/. By using the content of this publication, you agree to be bound by the terms of this license. For attribution, translations, adaptations, and permissions, please read the provisions and terms of use at https://www.adb.org/terms-use#openaccess.

This CC license does not apply to non-ADB copyright materials in this publication. If the material is attributed to another source, please contact the copyright owner or publisher of that source for permission to reproduce it. ADB cannot be held liable for any claims that arise as a result of your use of the material.

Please contact pubsmarketing@adb.org if you have questions or comments with respect to content, or if you wish to obtain copyright permission for your intended use that does not fall within these terms, or for permission to use the ADB logo.

Corrigenda to ADB publications may be found at http://www.adb.org/publications/corrigenda.

Notes:
In this publication, "₹" refers to Indian rupees, "$" to United States dollars, and "HK$" to Hong Kong dollars.
ADB recognizes "China" as the People's Republic of China, "Russia" as the Russian Federation, and "Bangalore" as Bengaluru.

On the cover: The Mumbai Metro is an ambitious project that aims to provide residents in and around the Mumbai Metropolitan Region a modern, fast, safe, and comfortable transport option that is accessible to all (photos from Shutterstock.com).

Contents

Table, Figures, and Maps	v
From the Commissioner's Desk	vii
Foreword	ix
Acknowledgments	xi
Abbreviations	xii
Weights and Measures	xiii
Executive Summary	xv
Transporting through Mumbai's History	**1**
A Brief History of Mumbai	1
Evolution of Public Transport	3
From an Island City to the Mumbai Metropolitan Area—The Journey of the Last 100 Years	4
Current Transportation Challenges in Mumbai	7
Breathing New Life into Mumbai	**13**
Mumbai Metro Master Plan	13
Project Progress	18
Contributing toward an Equitable City	**21**
Income Inequality in our Society—A Global and National Perspective	21
Existing Socioeconomic Profile of the Mumbai Metropolitan Region	23
Projected Changes in the Profile of the Mumbai Metropolitan Region	27
How the Mumbai Metro Can Empower through Equal Access for All	29
Contributing toward a Safer City	**37**
Passenger Safety—Life on the Lifeline	37
Mumbai Monsoons—A Transport Challenge	40
How the Mumbai Metro Can Provide a Safe Transport Option	41

Contributing toward a Cleaner City	**45**
Air Pollution in Mumbai—A Global Perspective	45
Major $PM_{2.5}$ Red Zones within Mumbai	46
Biggest Contributor to $PM_{2.5}$ in Mumbai	47
How the Mumbai Metro Can Reduce Air Pollution in Mumbai	49
Financial Sustainability	**53**
Financial Performance of Line 1	53
Financial Projections of Lines 2 and 7	54
Alternate Sources for Improving Financial Sustainability	56
Lessons from Other Metro Systems	**59**
Delhi Metro—Providing Equal Access to Everyone, Everywhere	59
Manila Metro Rail Transit System—Providing a Transport Alternative in a Densely Populated and Highly Polluted City	63
Rail + Property Model—Providing Financial Sustainability for Hong Kong, China Metro	65
Public Transportation in the COVID-19 Era	**69**
Behavioral Shifts and Patterns Expected Due to COVID-19	69
Conclusion	**73**
A New Era for Public Transportation in Mumbai	73

Table, Figures, and Maps

Table

E1	Comparison of Metro Network Coverage across Indian Cities	xvi

Figures

E1	Value for Money Framework for Assessing Urban Transport Infrastructure Projects	xvii
1	Growing Population and Changing Population Distribution in Greater Mumbai, 1901–2011	5
2	Changes in the Population Distribution in Different Parts of the Mumbai Metropolitan Region, 1971–2011	6
3	Spatial Coverage (in Terms of Area) within the Mumbai Metropolitan Region	7
4	Current Modal Share of Public Transport in Mumbai	8
5	Global Comparison of Average Speeds and Congestion Levels in Mumbai	10
6	Decreasing Share of Overall Public Transport (All Forms) over the Years in Mumbai	10
7	Average Commuter Distance Using the Different Modes of Transport in Mumbai	14
8	Details of the Mumbai Metro Master Plan	16
9	Evolution of Lines 1, 2, 3 and 7 of the Mumbai Metro	17
10	Completion Timelines of the Various Mumbai Metro Lines	18
11	Scatter Plot of Gini Coefficients and Gross Domestic Products of Selected Countries	21
12	Key Socioeconomic Indicators of Vulnerable Groups in the Mumbai Metropolitan Region	23
13	Employment Contribution of Various Sectors in the Mumbai Metropolitan Region	26
14	Comparison of Land Use Patterns in the Mumbai Metropolitan Region, 2016 and 2036	27
15	Bubble Chart of Gross Domestic Products, Population, and Business Employment in Key Cities of the World in 2030	28
16	Bubble Chart of Gross Domestic Products, Population, and Secondary Employment in Key Cities of the World in 2030	29
17	Results of Commuter Satisfaction Survey for Mumbai Metro Line 1, 2014	33
18	Time Benefit (from Better Accessibility) Due to Metro Lines 2A, 2B, and 7 and Benefit Realization Time Frame, 2021–2051	34
19	Normal Curve Plot of Country-Wise Road Traffic Deaths per Annum	37
20	Scatter Plot of Risk Exposure on Indian Roads	38
21	Total Number of Railway Accident Deaths on the Mumbai Suburban Railway Network, 2010–2015	39
22	Safety Features Provided by the Mumbai Metro Trains	42
23	Benefit from Reduction in Road and Rail Accidents Due to Metro Lines 2A, 2B, and 7 and Benefit Realization Time Frame, 2021–2051	43
24	Normal Curve Plot of Mean Annual Exposure of $PM_{2.5}$ of Selected Cities in the World	45
25	Contribution of Transport Emissions to $PM_{2.5}$ Particles in Mumbai, 2018 and 2030	47
26	Increasing Trend of Cars per Capita in Mumbai, 2001–2017	48
27	Projected Mega-Cities (by Population) of India in 2030	49

28	Changes in Transportation Modal Shares After the Introduction of the Mumbai Metro	50
29	Environmental Benefits Due to Lines 2A, 2B, 7 and Benefit Realization Time Frame, 2021–2051	51
30	Annual Revenue and Operating Expenditure of Mumbai Metro Line 1, 2015–2019	53
31	Operating Expenditure Components of Mumbai Metro Line 1, 2015–2019	54
32	Capital Expenditure and Revenue Projections of Lines 2 and 7 Combined, 2018–2050	55
33	Distance-Wise Fare Comparison of Public Transport Modes with Proposed Fares of Metro Lines 2 and 7	55
34	Accessibility to All Due to the Delhi Metro, with the Key National Capital Region Industrial Centers	60
35	Accessibility to All Due to the Delhi Metro, with the Key National Capital Region Commercial Centers	61
36	Accessibility to All Due to the Delhi Metro, with the Key National Capital Region Health-Care and Education Centers	62
37	Parametric Comparison of Manila with Mumbai	63
38	Data Analysis for $PM_{2.5}$ Risk Exposure via Different Modes of Public Transport in Manila	65
39	Overall Revenue of Mass Transit Railway Corporation (Hong Kong, China) and Contribution of Real Estate-Driven Revenue, 2010–2019	65
40	Key Stakeholders in the Rail + Property Model in Hong Kong, China	66
41	Key Success Factors for the Rail + Property Model in Hong Kong, China	67
42	Key Urban Mobility-Related COVID-19 Trends	70

Maps

E1	The Mumbai Metropolitan Region	xvi
1	Cluster of Seven Islands in Erstwhile Bombay	1
2	Consolidation of the Seven Islands	2
3	Heat Map of Expansion of Mumbai to the Modern-Day Mumbai Metropolitan Area, 1973–2014	5
4	Area-Wise Employment per Working Population in the Mumbai Metropolitan Region by District	8
5	Comparison of Metro Rail Transit System Coverage around the World	11
6	Traffic Flow Pattern of the Two Zones of the Indian Railways	13
7	Mumbai Metro Master Plan	15
8	Normal Curve Plot of State-Wise Gini Coefficients in India	22
9	Slum Clusters in Greater Mumbai	25
10	Key Education Institutes Close to the Alignment of the Mumbai Metro Master Plan	31
11	Key Health-Care Facilities Close to the Alignment of the Mumbai Metro Master Plan	32
12	Heat Map of Major $PM_{2.5}$ Red Zones in Mumbai	46

From the Commissioner's Desk

The Mumbai Metro is a marquee project that will improve the overall quality of the Mumbai Metropolitan Region transport based on the Comprehensive Transport Study done by the Mumbai Metropolitan Region Development Authority (MMRDA). We are focused on completing 337 kilometers of metro lines in Mumbai by year 2026 so that fellow Mumbaikars can reach anywhere in the Mumbai Metropolitan Region from any place within 60 minutes. We are proactively focused on meeting the deadline while also trying to minimize the temporary inconvenience caused to Mumbaikars due to such projects.

Presently, 11 million passengers use public transport in Mumbai daily. During peak hours, the super-dense-crush-load conditions on the existing suburban trains tend to be in the range of 12–16 persons per square meter. Our studies also suggest that road congestion level is almost 97% in different parts and, thus, average vehicle speeds are not more than 10–12 km/hour in the city. Such extreme conditions can lead to unsafe travel in the buses and on suburban trains in Mumbai. We are sure that the metro will reduce congestion, not only on roads but also on the suburban trains. Once completed, the 337-kilometer metro rail, will also create capacity for transporting more than 12 million passengers daily. Hence, the metro will offer almost twice the capacity with double comfort (at 6 persons per square meter). It will also provide faster transit speeds and better accessibility from work and residential spaces.

It gives me immense pride to say that we, at the MMRDA, are putting all efforts in long-term solutions that will improve the quality of life of the people in Mumbai. It is important to mention that we have constantly received a lot of support from the Government of Maharashtra and the Government of India, which has further helped us to take faster decisions. We, in partnership with the Asian Development Bank (ADB), promise to continue to offer a transparent and responsive organization to the people of Mumbai while continuing to remain in constant contact with the citizens to provide better services to them. I would like to thank ADB and the other development partners who have been helping us on this journey to transform the Mumbai Metropolitan Region.

I hope that this booklet will serve as a platform for strengthening and coordinating action in support of the Mumbai Metro and help in realizing the vision of "Mumbai in Minutes."

S.V.R. Srinivas, Indian Administrative Service
Metropolitan Commissioner
Mumbai Metropolitan Region Development Authority

Foreword

The idea behind this book is to tell a story of the future of public transport in Mumbai. Mumbai is the financial capital of India and one of India's largest metropolitan areas. However, it is also one of the most densely populated cities in the world, having extreme pressure on its existing infrastructure. To enable the city to develop to its full potential, it needs to add capacity in its public transport infrastructure focusing on a safe and comfortable transport option.

The Mumbai Metro is a large and ambitious project that will transform public transportation in and around Mumbai. It will provide easy and equal access to everyone across the city. Not only will it relieve the pressure on the overutilized existing modes of transport, i.e., suburban railway and buses, but it also provide a safer and cleaner transport alternative. The project is also expected to have wider benefits such as facilitating comprehensive metropolitan development via the creation of multimodal urban transport networks, promoting systematic urban land use planning, and attracting private sector investments. It will incentivize transit-oriented development schemes and support financial sustainability through value-capture financing initiatives.

The new metro lines will offer an opportunity to create a modern public transport system with innovative safety and technology features for the people in Mumbai. The Asian Development Bank (ADB) takes pride in signing a $926 million loan for the Mumbai Metro with the Government of India. ADB financing will ease travel for millions of commuters across Mumbai and decongest heavily crowded suburban rail systems. But more than just a solution to Mumbai's transportation needs, this project is a means to reshape Mumbai City into a modern, clean, and more livable city for all its inhabitants.

The metro will have various features that will benefit women, such as women-only carriages, mobile applications for women's security, and separate ticket counters. The connectivity and accessibility provided by the metro will ensure that women and differently abled passengers have improved opportunities for employment. There will also be station and carriage facilities for the elderly and differently abled passengers, including priority e-ticket counters.

ADB is committed to achieve a prosperous, inclusive, and sustainable India and Asia by focusing on projects that improve the quality of public transport while reducing the environmental impact. The Mumbai Metro will reduce carbon dioxide emissions from vehicles by about 166,000 tons per annum because of the shift of passengers to the metro.

I sincerely appreciate the officials of the Mumbai Metropolitan Region Development Authority for being at the helm to implement this challenging project. Besides the core team led by Sharad Saxena, principal transport specialist, this publication benefited from contributions of several persons, including project officers of ADB and project beneficiaries. I thank all of them.

I hope this book will be read widely by those interested in Mumbai's and India's future, and in urban transport in general. I wish this book helps to generate further efforts in providing a world-class, well-integrated public transport system to all people in the Mumbai Metropolitan Region.

Kenichi Yokoyama
Director General
South Asia Department
Asian Development Bank

Acknowledgments

The Transport and Communications Division of the South Asia Department (SARD), Asian Development Bank (ADB), produced this publication.

Sharad Saxena, principal transport specialist, led the task team and steered the production of the publication, assisted by Cheska Llamas and Cynthia Gutierrez. Abhishek Kaushal and Rajaji Meshram (staff consultants) undertook research and initial write-up, and helped structure the report, including rounding up of photos and graphics for illustration. James Leather and Kirsty Rowan Marcus provided valuable comments, technical insights on content, and overall guidance.

ADB's SARD Director General Kenichi Yokoyama, Director Ravi Peri of South Asia Transport and Communications, and Country Director Takeo Konishi of the India Resident Mission provided constant guidance, direction, and support.

This publication was possible with the participation and support of the Government of India's Ministry of Finance, Department of Economic Affairs, and the Mumbai Metropolitan Region Development Authority.

The Publishing team of ADB's Department of Communications handled the production and coordination of this publication, while the Printing Unit of the Corporate Services Department provided printing assistance.

Dedication

In memory of Bharat Modgil, senior director of the Mumbai Metropolitan Region Development Authority. B. Modgil retired as general manager of the Central Railway and was the chief executive officer of Mumbai Metro Line 1, which is already operational.

Abbreviations

ADB	Asian Development Bank
BDA	Bangalore Development Authority
BEST	Brihanmumbai Electricity Supply and Transport
BRICS	Brazil, Russian Federation, India, People's Republic of China, and South Africa
COVID-19	coronavirus disease
FAR	floor area ratio
GDP	gross domestic product
MMOPL	Mumbai Metro One Private Limited
MMR	Mumbai Metropolitan Region
MMRDA	Mumbai Metropolitan Region Development Authority
MTR	mass transit railway
MTRC	Mass Transit Railway Corporation
NCR	National Capital Region
PM	particulate matter
$PM_{2.5}$	particulate matter with 2.5 microns in diameter or smaller
WHO	World Health Organization

Weights and Measures

µg	microgram
km	kilometer
km^2	square kilometer
m^3	cubic meter

Executive Summary

The purpose of this book is to highlight the crucial role the Mumbai Metro is expected to play in the overall development of the Mumbai Metropolitan Region (MMR). This book explains how the development of the metro rail transit system will enable Mumbai (and thus the MMR) to become a more equitable, safer, and cleaner place. It also assesses how other global metro systems have significantly contributed to making their respective cities more equitable, cleaner, and safer.

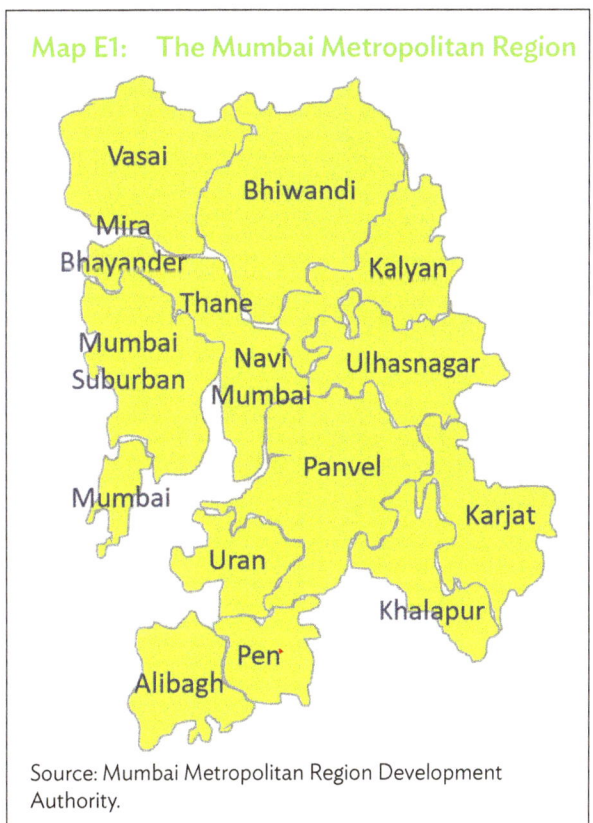

Map E1: The Mumbai Metropolitan Region

Source: Mumbai Metropolitan Region Development Authority.

Mumbai has undergone several changes in the 20th and 21st centuries to become India's financial capital. As India's most famous business hub, it has attracted large volumes of people seeking employment and has grown from the Island City of 157 square kilometers (km^2) to the modern-day sprawl of 6,355 km^2 (Map E1). The influx of people has increased the MMR population to more than 12.5 million. This has created a unique set of challenges for one of the world's most densely populated cities. Presently, while most of the jobs are in central Mumbai, most of the population resides in Mumbai Suburban and surrounding districts within the MMR. Currently, people in the MMR rely heavily on the Mumbai suburban railway for commuting to work daily.

Mumbai suburban rail is the lifeline of Mumbai City and has a modal share of 43%, followed by the Brihanmumbai Electricity Supply and Transport (BEST) buses at 20%. However, with the increasing population in Mumbai, as well as the surrounding areas within the MMR, the pressure on the existing transport infrastructure has also been increasing. The suburban trains transport close to 5,000 people per 9-coach train against a design capacity of 1,750 people, making the Mumbai suburban railway one of most crowded public transport systems in the world.

Meanwhile, the state-owned BEST bus system operates on roads with a congestion index of 34 (proximity to zero indicates "no congestion"), which is significantly higher than that of leading cities in the world such as New York, Tokyo, London, and Shanghai. Because of this, the overall share of public transport in Mumbai (covering all modes) has been gradually decreasing over the last few decades, dropping from 88% in 1991 to 65% in 2020.

Table E1: Comparison of Metro Network Coverage across Indian Cities

City	Operational kilometer per million people
Bangalore	3.0
Chennai	4.0
Delhi	12.0
Hyderabad	7.0
Kolkata	2.0
Lucknow	6.0
Mumbai	0.5
Pune	8.0

Source: Official websites of respective metro corporations.

Existing transport modes like the suburban rail system have been undertaking several capacity enhancements, such as signaling improvement, introduction of 12-coach trains, extending the lengths of all platforms, patch doubling and tripling, etc. However, due to limited additional availability of land, any further capacity enhancement is restricted. Thus, there is a need for an alternative mode of mass public transportation to encourage mode shift back from private vehicles. Several cities in India have already constructed and operationalized metro systems to boost public transport and commuter convenience. However, the current metro network coverage for Mumbai is extremely low (Table E1).

Currently, this index is very low for Mumbai since only one metro line is operational. However, the metro coverage in Mumbai is expected to improve strongly with the realization of the Mumbai Metro Master Plan developed by the Mumbai Metropolitan Region Development Authority (Map 7). At present, only Line 1 is operational, while Lines 2A, 2B, 3, 4, 6, and 7 are at different stages of construction.

All lines of the Mumbai Metro are projected to be completed by 2026. The Mumbai Metro is expected to greatly benefit the city of Mumbai as well as the MMR by improving urban transport safety and comfort for the residents, especially for the poor and the vulnerable. It is also expected to provide enhanced access to economic opportunities and social service facilities in Mumbai.

It is important to understand the benefits generated by the Mumbai Metro. Modern assessment of urban transport infrastructure projects has shifted from a purely financial to a more holistic model of evaluation. The core of this assessment framework considers that, since taxpayers' money is mostly used in such projects, the project should maximize the benefits generated for the public. These benefits cannot be just financial in nature, and they need to have an overall improvement in the quality of life of the taxpayers. This assessment framework is known as the value for money, which has become widely accepted for urban transportation infrastructure projects. The value for money aims to understand how a variety of factors such as social, economic, and environmental, in addition to financial, can make the quality of life of the public better, as shown in Figure E1.

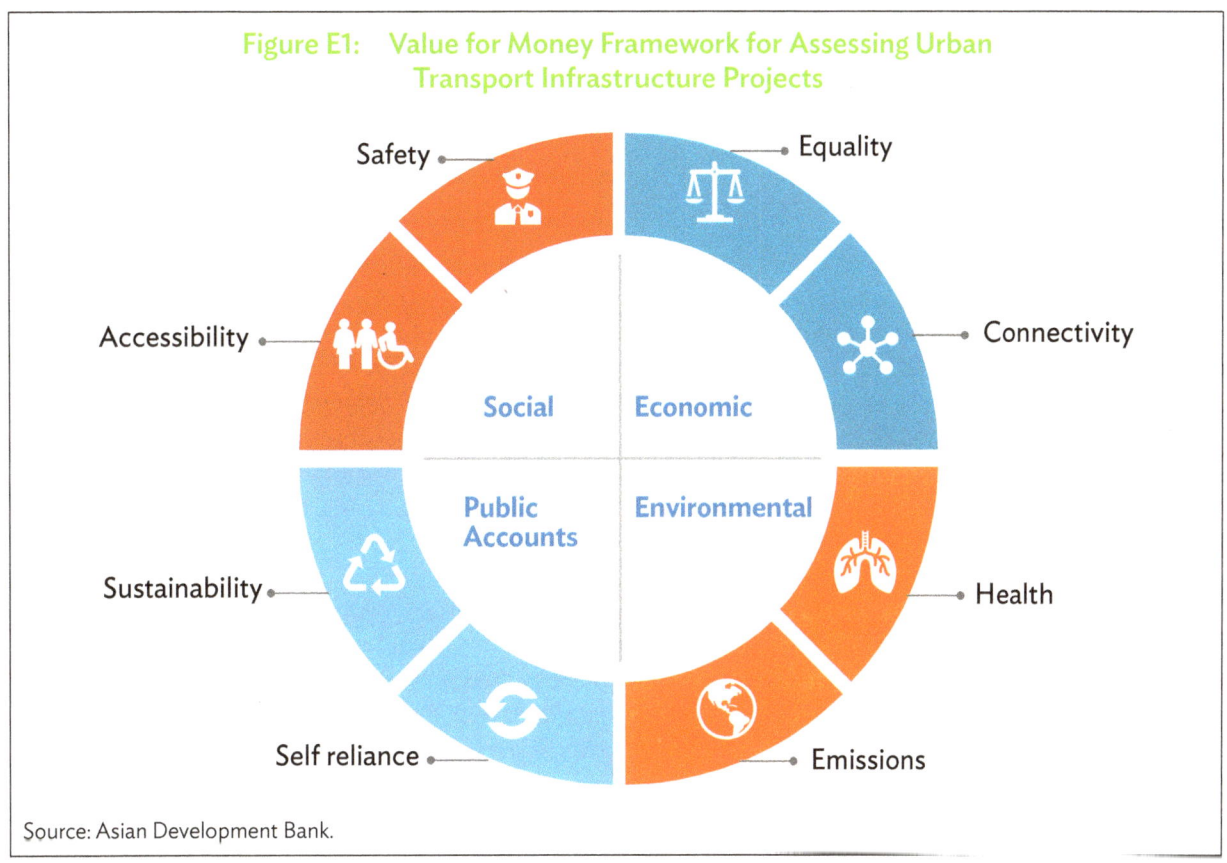

Figure E1: Value for Money Framework for Assessing Urban Transport Infrastructure Projects

Source: Asian Development Bank.

From an equity point of view, strong measures need to be undertaken within India and Maharashtra to bridge the socioeconomic gap between different social groups. Since the MMR is the biggest contributor to Maharashtra's gross domestic product, uplifting its vulnerable groups needs to be emphasized. The vulnerable groups in Mumbai include the low-income workers, women, and the differently abled. Of the total population in the MMR, 28% lives in slum areas. Further, Mumbai has a female work participation percentage of only 18%, while 3% of the population is differently abled. The Mumbai Metro can empower these groups with equal access to all parts of the region. The provision of surveillance cameras inside trains and at every metro station, along with facilities and services aimed at women (nursing and breastfeeding room facilities at each station, separate hygienic toilets at each station, sanitary pad dispensing machines, separate ticket counters and vending machines, allocated spaces in metro stations owned or operated by women, dedicated carriages for women passengers, dedicated seats for women in each coach), and the differently abled (access ramps, escalators and elevators, dedicated seats for the differently abled in each coach) are expected to support these groups. The Mumbai Metro is foreseen to further support these groups by providing equitable access to important centers of socioeconomic development, such as schools and colleges, hospitals, employment hubs, industrial areas, etc.

With more than 150,000 road-traffic deaths recorded per annum (i.e., the highest number per annum in the world), understanding the safety conditions on the rail and road networks in India is important. Even the number of road-traffic deaths relative to population is high in India compared with developed countries, as well as the nations of Brazil, Russian Federation, India, People's Repulic of China, and South Africa (BRICS). In fact, Mumbai is in the top 10 of unsafe cities in India for road-based transportation, despite its relatively higher patronage of public transportation. There is also a high number of railway fatalities per annum, even though 43% of commuters in Mumbai use public transit to travel. The 5-year period ending in 2015 resulted in more than 11 deaths per day on the Mumbai suburban network. The biggest contributor to rail-related deaths is trespassing (82%), followed by people falling from moving trains (18%). Trespassing incidents are high because of unauthorized crossing of the suburban railway tracks, which are entirely at grade. The incidents of people falling from moving trains are high since the suburban trains do not have doors (by design) and thus allow desperate commuters to hang onto the already overcrowded trains in order to reach their destination.

The problem on safety while commuting is aggravated by the Mumbai monsoons. The heavy rains of more than 2,000 millimeters per annum inundate the railway tracks and roads, and lead to issues like train delays, train derailments, and even cancellations of services, leaving thousands of commuters stranded frequently during these months. The Mumbai Metro is expected to solve these problems in its very design. The metro tracks in Mumbai will be either elevated or underground, thereby deterring trespassers from the tracks. Further, the metro trains will have doors that close as soon as the train starts moving. This should deter people from hanging outside the trains. Additional elements like platform screen doors should prevent people from accidentally being pushed onto the tracks while waiting for the trains. Importantly, the elevated tracks of the metro rail transit system can ensure that the metro is able to operate continuously even in the monsoons, despite the occurrence of waterlogging at the ground level.

In addition to safety, the Mumbai Metro will also have several facilities for providing improved accessibility to the vulnerable groups including the low income, women, and the differently abled. The metro lines will empower the vulnerable groups in Mumbai with better accessibility to a number of socioeconomic centers of development, such as education institutes and health-care facilities, in a comfortable manner. This accessibility will enable the people of the MMR to easily use these facilities and eventually improve the key socioeconomic indexes like literacy, health, and employment. This improved accessibility will be critical given the projected changes in land use patterns of urban as well as industrial areas, where more and more areas outside the confines of Mumbai City will undergo enhanced economic activity.

From an environmental point of view, Mumbai is in the top five most polluted cities in the world, having an annual measure of 64 micrograms per cubic meter ($\mu g/m^3$) in particulate matter with at most 2.5 microns in diameter ($PM_{2.5}$). This $PM_{2.5}$ measure is more than three times the world average of 18 $\mu g/m^3$ and more than 6 times the safe limit prescribed by the World Health Organization at 10 $\mu g/m^3$. The two biggest contributors toward $PM_{2.5}$ in Mumbai are industrial emissions (42%) and transport emissions (26%). However, it is expected that transport emissions will become the biggest contributor to $PM_{2.5}$ by 2030, with a 35% share. The number of private vehicles per 1,000 people has increased more than 3 times since 2001 in Mumbai. All these factors are contributing toward higher $PM_{2.5}$ levels; although, the introduction of the Mumbai Metro is expected to significantly change this trend. Currently, 43% of people in Mumbai commute using the Mumbai suburban rail system, while 35% use motorized vehicles. Only 2% of the population currently use the metro (and the monorail). However, the modal share of the metro (and monorail) is expected to increase to 36% by 2031 and thus reduce the share of motorized vehicles from 35% to 24%. This reduction in motorized vehicles is eventually expected to control the growing $PM_{2.5}$ emissions and make Mumbai a cleaner city for everyone.

Mumbai Metro is focusing on leveraging non-fare revenue sources for improving the financial sustainability of the project. The Government of Maharashtra increased the stamp duty from 5% to 6% in 2018, applicable to all property transactions in Mumbai. Proceeds from this would finance major transport infrastructure projects currently being undertaken in the MMR. But in March 2020, because of the coronavirus disease (COVID-19), the government announced a concession for 2 years in this stamp duty increase to boost the construction and realty sectors in Mumbai. Other value-capture financing instruments considered include the increase in development charges by 100% and a transit-oriented development policy that allows for additional purchasable floor area ratio on payment of a premium, where 50% of this premium is proposed to be dedicated toward financing of the metro rail transit system.

Overall, the realization of the Mumbai Metro Master Plan can herald a new era for public transportation in Mumbai. The Mumbai Metro will provide easy and equal access to everyone across the city. It will not only reduce the pressure on the existing suburban railway and buses, but also enhance safety. The metro system in Mumbai can strongly contribute to a modern and safe rail-based urban transit system that will improve the overall quality of the city's transport system.

The subsequent chapters detail how the Mumbai Metro can make Mumbai a more equitable, safer, and cleaner city.

The Gateway of India. The erstwhile Bombay was a critical trading city in the British Empire (photo by TRphotos/Shutterstock.com).

Transporting through Mumbai's History

A Brief History of Mumbai

The former city of Bombay (present day Mumbai) was originally inhabited by the Kolis, a local fishing community. It came under the control of the Portuguese during the 1500s, as they realized the potential of the city to be a direct gateway to India due to its natural deep-water harbor. At that time, Bombay was an archipelago separated by swampy lands and consisting of seven islands (Map 1): Bombay, Colaba, Mahim, Mazagaon, Little Colaba (also known as Old Woman's Island), Parel, and Worli.

Map 1:   Cluster of Seven Islands in Erstwhile Bombay

Source: TIFR and Nichalp. 2008. The Seven Islands of Bombay. *Wikimedia Commons*.

In 1661, the seven islands were handed over to England by the Portuguese as a part of the dowry of Catherine of Braganza when she married Charles II. At this point, the city was rechristened as the Island City and had an approximate population of 10,000. Due to its natural advantage of a deep-water harbor, the Island City soon became a center of trade in India. This led to the economic growth and industrialization of the Island City. The city had an active shipbuilding business, enhancing its economy from export of cotton and import of textiles. This provided a great opportunity for people from different trades and specialties, such as goldsmiths, weavers, ironsmiths, planters, merchants, moneylenders, and servants, to come and work in the Island City.

In the early 1800s, significant engineering work was carried out in Bombay to support the increasing population. Several construction projects were undertaken during this period, such as the introduction of railways in 1853, the introduction of the Municipal Corporation of Bombay in 1872, etc. Several land reclamation projects were also undertaken by authorities to fill the city swamps and combine the seven islands into one consolidated landmass. By 1845, the seven small islands were merged to form one large island known as Bombay (Map 2).

Map 2: Consolidation of the Seven Islands

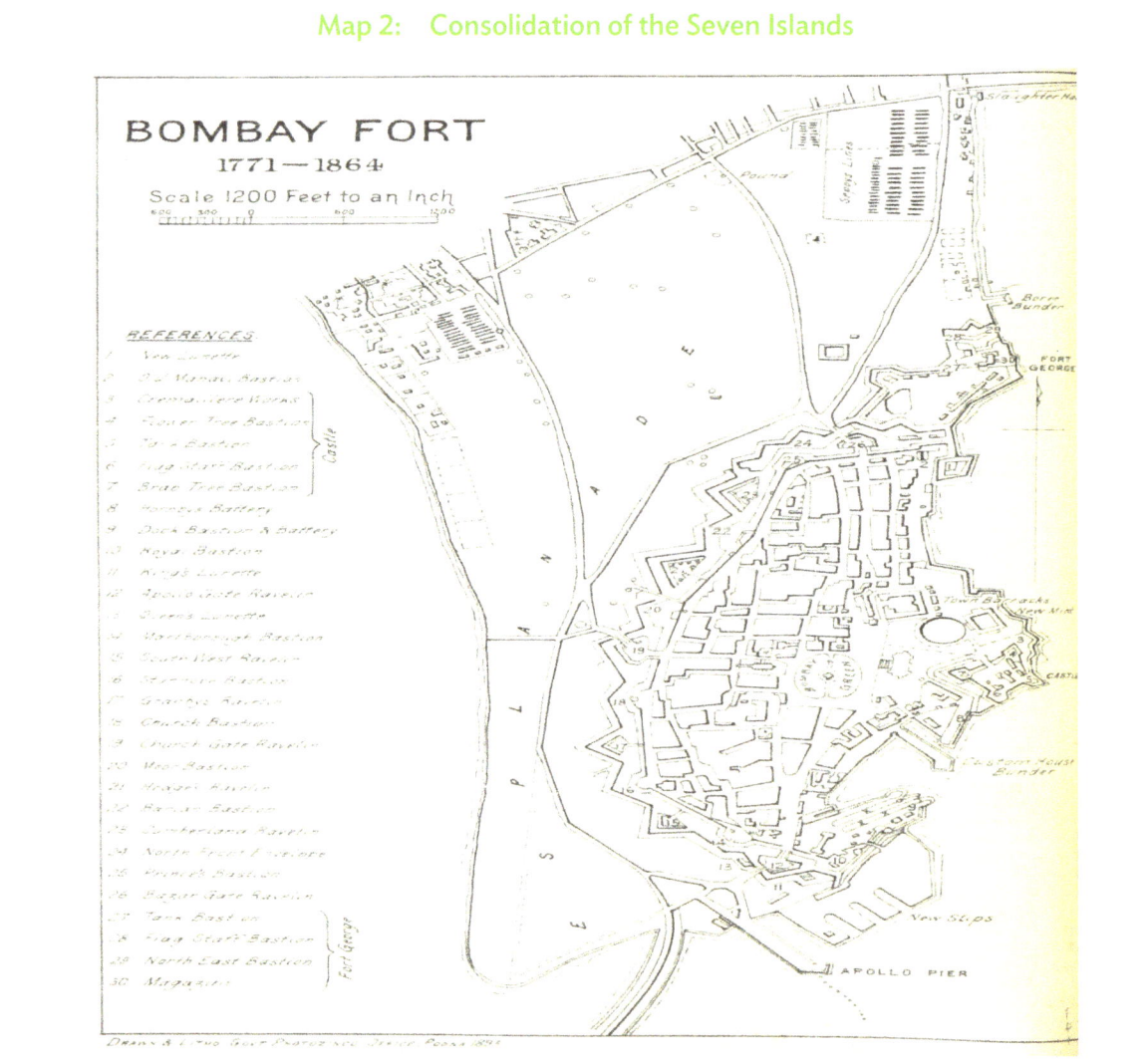

Source: Image credits to British Library Digitized Catalogue from R. E. Enthoven. 1896. General Index. In J. M. Campbell, ed. *Gazetteer of the Bombay Presidency*. Bombay: Government Central Press. p. 16.

During the civil war in America, India became the main supplier of raw cotton to England, with large volumes exported from Bombay. Bombay witnessed an extraordinary increase in industrial and trade activities leading to strong commercial growth during this period. Many industries, primarily textile mills, were set up in the city during the 19th century, and Bombay became a textile hub. India's first cotton mill, the Bombay Spinning Mill, was also set up in the city in 1854. By 1864, more than 100 companies were registered in Bombay, operating as banks, financial associations, land companies, press companies, shipping companies, insurance companies, and joint stock companies. Businesses boomed as money flooded into the city during this period, and the population of the city increased rapidly to around 0.8 million by 1864.

Evolution of Public Transport

Railways were introduced for the first time in Bombay in 1853, between Victoria Terminus and Thane. The 33-kilometer (km) long railway line was the first passenger railway in India. The city was later connected to other major Indian cities. In 1870, railway lines from Bombay (present day Mumbai) to Madras (present day Chennai) and from Bombay to Calcutta (present day Kolkata) were also built.

In 1872, the Municipal Corporation of Bombay was established to understand the problems and requirements of the city. It added new modes of public transport to replace the existing methods, such as carts or carriages drawn by animals.

Mula River in Dapoorie near Poona, circa 1858. A passenger train connecting Bombay to Thane traversed the Dapoorie Viaduct (photo from the British Library online gallery).

The Bombay Tramway Company Limited began tramways operations in the city in 1873. Initially, these trams were pulled by horses; however, horse-drawn trams were considered slow and expensive and failed to attract citizens.

After a few years, in 1907, electric tramways were introduced and were well received. These were operated by the Brihanmumbai Electricity Supply and Transport (BEST), formerly known as the Bombay Electric Supply and Tramways Company, which added new trams and also ran double-decker buses in the city. The BEST shut the tramway system in 1964, but it still operates bus services in Mumbai.

Bus transportation in Mumbai. The Brihanmumbai Electricity Supply and Transport (BEST) buses were an important mode of urban transport in the city since the early 1960s (photo by Nichalp in *Wikimedia Commons*).

From an Island City to the Mumbai Metropolitan Area—The Journey of the Last 100 Years

Mumbai has undergone several changes in the last century on its journey to becoming India's current business and financial hub. As illustrated in Map 3, it has spatially grown from the Island City of 157 square kilometers (km^2) to Greater Mumbai (437 km^2, including the suburbs of Andheri, Bandra, and Borivali) to eventually transform into the modern-day Mumbai Metropolitan Region (MMR) (6,355 km^2, including Thane, Navi Mumbai, Vasai-Virar, Mira Bhayander, among others). Today, the MMR contributes 6% of India's gross domestic product (GDP).[1]

---

[1] U. Adusumilli. 2016. *Role of Regional Development Institutions in Creating an Enabling Environment towards Shared Prosperity: The Case of Mumbai Metropolitan Region.* Presentation for the International Conference on Sustainable Development through Quality Infrastructure Investment. Tokyo. 20–21 January.

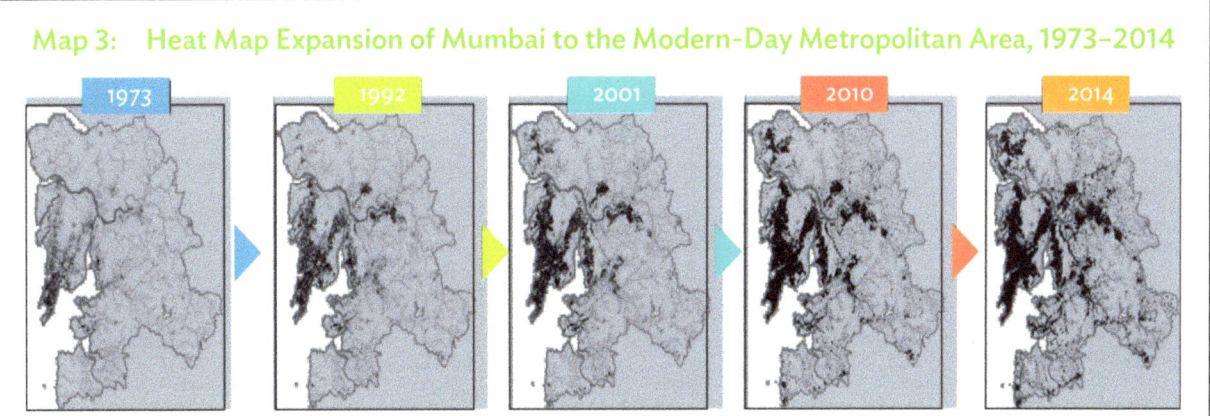

Map 3: Heat Map Expansion of Mumbai to the Modern-Day Metropolitan Area, 1973–2014

Source: S. Rawoot, J. L. Wescoat Jr., K. Noiva, and A. Marks. 2015. *Mumbai Case Study*. Product of research on Enhancing Blue-Green Environmental and Social Performance in High Density Urban Environments (sponsored by the Ramboll Foundation). Cambridge, MA: Massachusetts Institute of Technology.

A study of the historical population growth in various parts of the modern-day MMR reveals the key changes that have given it its current shape. More than 100 years ago, Greater Mumbai, having a population of 0.9 million, was one of most important trade centers in India. As depicted in Figure 1, in 1901, its population share (84%) was heavily skewed toward the Island City. Only 16% of the population resided in the modern-day suburbs of Greater Mumbai. Today, almost 75% of the current population of 12.5 million in Greater Mumbai live in the suburbs and only 25% stay in the Island City.[2]

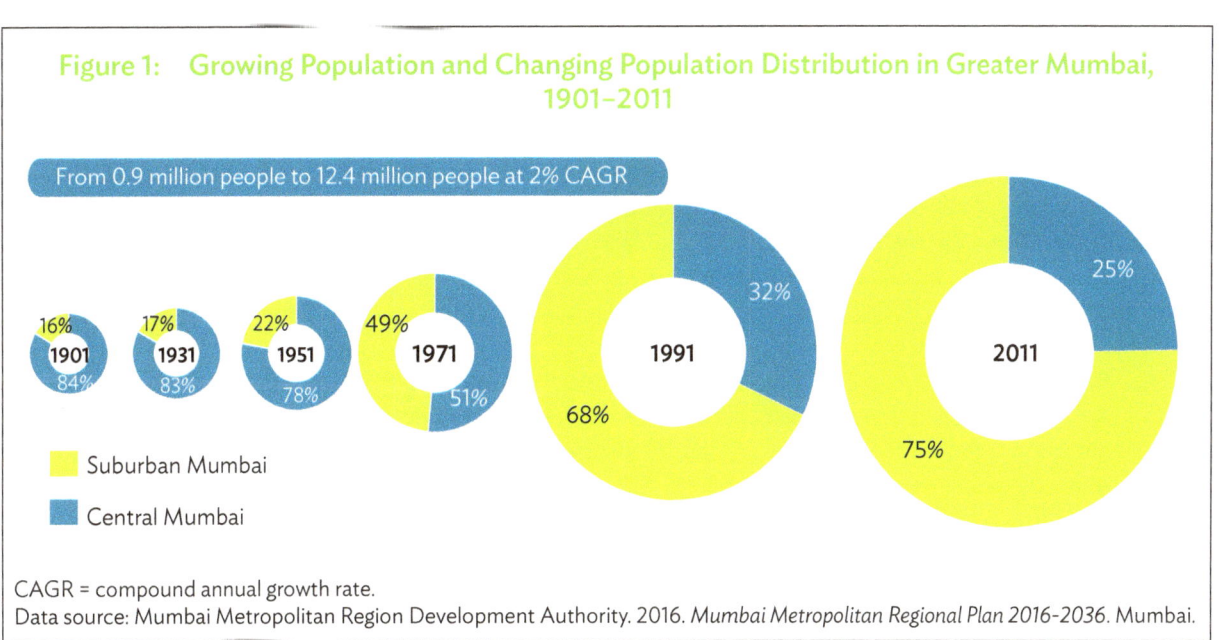

Figure 1: Growing Population and Changing Population Distribution in Greater Mumbai, 1901–2011

CAGR = compound annual growth rate.
Data source: Mumbai Metropolitan Region Development Authority. 2016. *Mumbai Metropolitan Regional Plan 2016-2036*. Mumbai.

---

[2] Mumbai Metropolitan Region Development Authority. 2016. *Mumbai Metropolitan Regional Plan 2016-2036*. Mumbai.

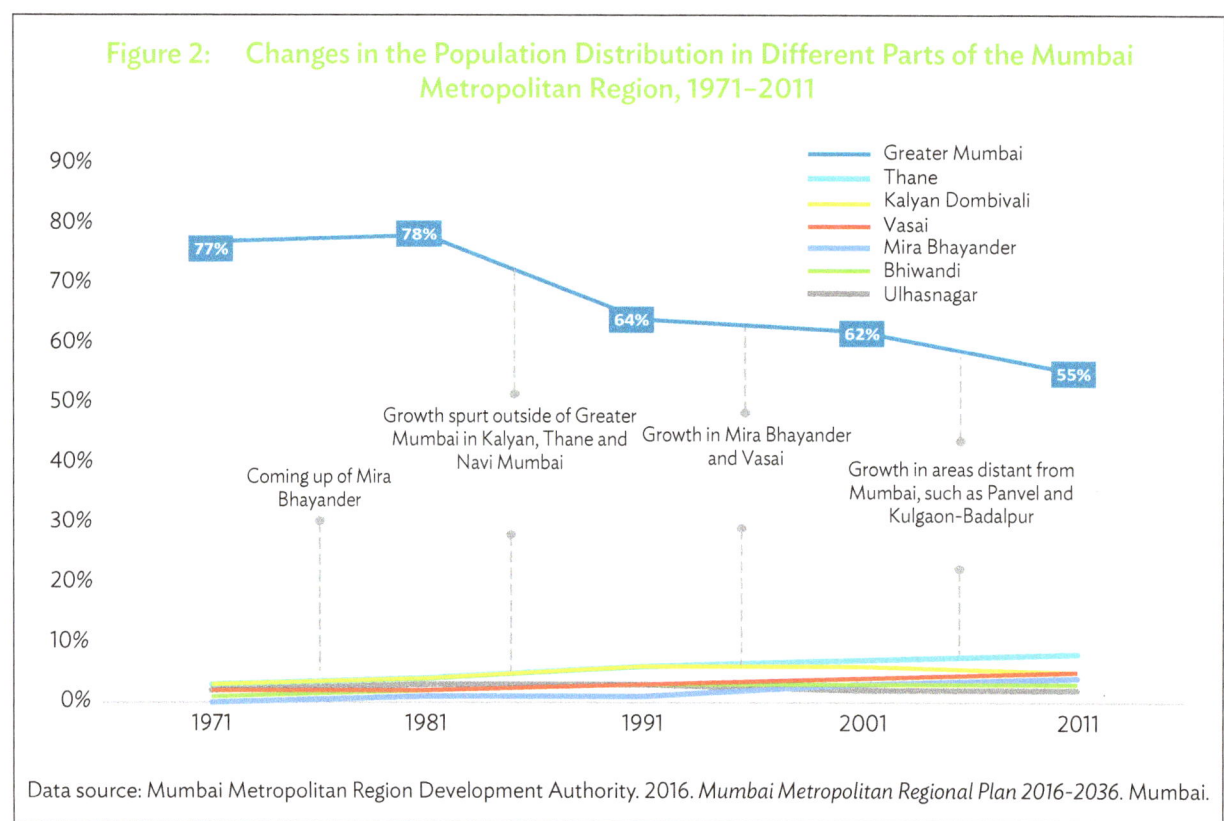

Figure 2: Changes in the Population Distribution in Different Parts of the Mumbai Metropolitan Region, 1971–2011

Data source: Mumbai Metropolitan Region Development Authority. 2016. *Mumbai Metropolitan Regional Plan 2016-2036*. Mumbai.

Over the last century, the population of Greater Mumbai increased by almost 12 times and the distribution of this population reversed, with a majority now residing in the suburbs of Greater Mumbai. This spurt of spatial growth to accommodate the increasing population spilled outside the boundaries of Greater Mumbai. The expansion started in the 1980s, with development in the surrounding areas of Thane and Kalyan-Dombivali (Figure 2). The trend of outward expansion of Greater Mumbai has gathered momentum ever since and, hence, the population share of Greater Mumbai in the modern-day MMR has fallen from 77% to 55% (footnote 2). This population shift has been driven by an upsurge in new areas around Greater Mumbai, with recent growth spurts being witnessed in distant areas like Panvel and Badalpur.

Today, all these areas combine to form the MMR, which consists of eight municipal corporations, nine municipal councils, and several villages. The area-wise contribution of the major municipal corporations and municipal councils that constitute the MMR is shown in Figure 3. In terms of area, the biggest part of the MMR is Greater Mumbai, which is its core.

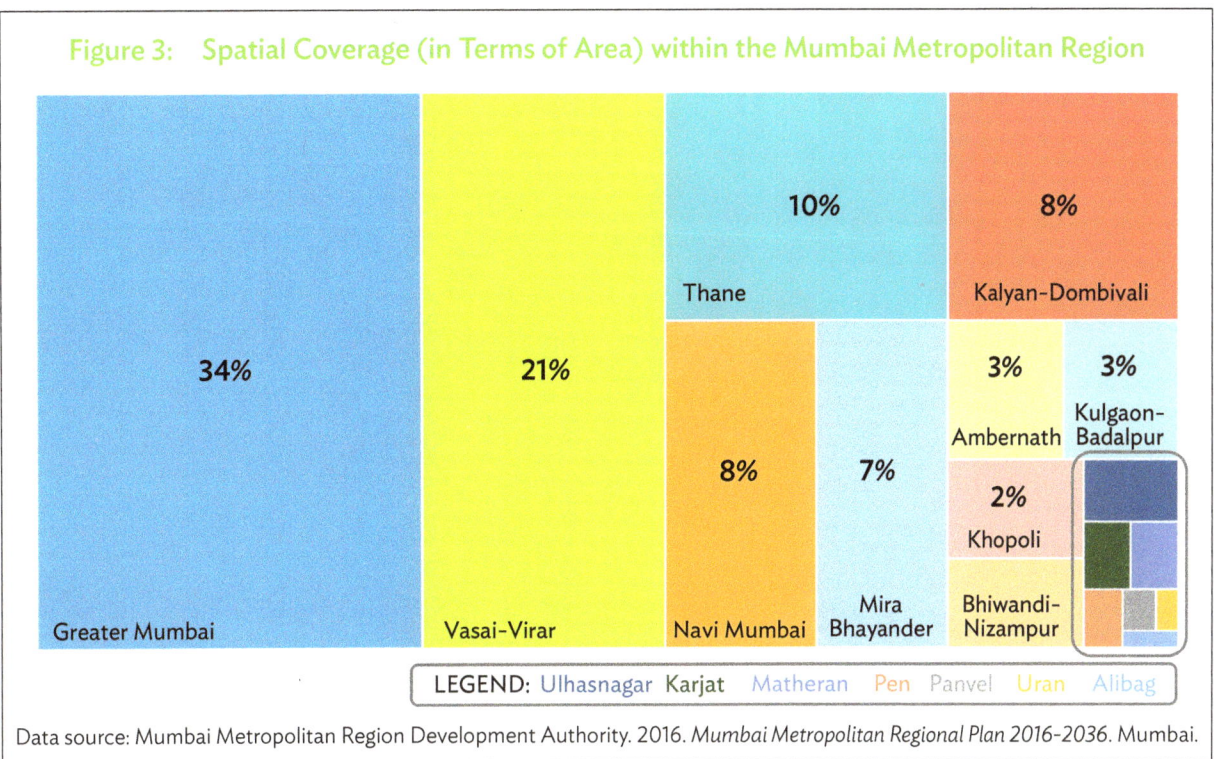

Figure 3: Spatial Coverage (in Terms of Area) within the Mumbai Metropolitan Region

Data source: Mumbai Metropolitan Region Development Authority. 2016. *Mumbai Metropolitan Regional Plan 2016-2036*. Mumbai.

Current Transportation Challenges in Mumbai

As observed previously, most of the population of Greater Mumbai (almost 75%) reside in the suburbs of Mumbai, with just 25% living in Mumbai City. However, the suburbs of Mumbai accommodate just 30% of the Greater Mumbai's factories, leading to a mismatch between the location of jobs and the location of the working population.[3] The metric of employment, with respect to the working population within each district, helps to identify the need of the working population to commute out of their respective districts for their daily jobs. A value of "more than 1" indicates that the people of the district will have a lesser probability of travelling outside their district for jobs. On the other hand, a value of "less than 1" indicates that the people within the district do not have sufficient employment opportunities within their respective districts.

Map 4 demonstrates how the metrics of employment per working population for areas surrounding Mumbai City—e.g., Mumbai Suburbs (0.23), Thane (0.42), Navi Mumbai (0.35), Mira Bhayander (0.35), and Vasai (0.34)—are significantly lesser than the metric of the city itself, which is relatively very high at a value of 1.62. Hence, people from the areas surrounding Mumbai City (with low metric values) need to travel all the way to Mumbai City for their daily jobs. These people need to cover longer distances to commute to work on a daily basis and thus rely on good transport systems.

As seen in Figure 4, there is a heavy reliance on public transport. Mumbai suburban rail captures the highest modal share at 43%, followed by the BEST buses at 20%.[4]

---

[3] H. Indorewala et al. 2017. *City Résumé—Mumbai*. Building Inclusive Urban Communities. Mumbai: Kamla Raheja Vidyanidhi Institute of Architecture and Environmental Studies.
[4] Municipal Corporation of Greater Mumbai. 2016. *Comprehensive Mobility Plan for Greater Mumbai*. Mumbai.

Map 4: Area-Wise Employment per Working Population in the Mumbai Metropolitan Region by District

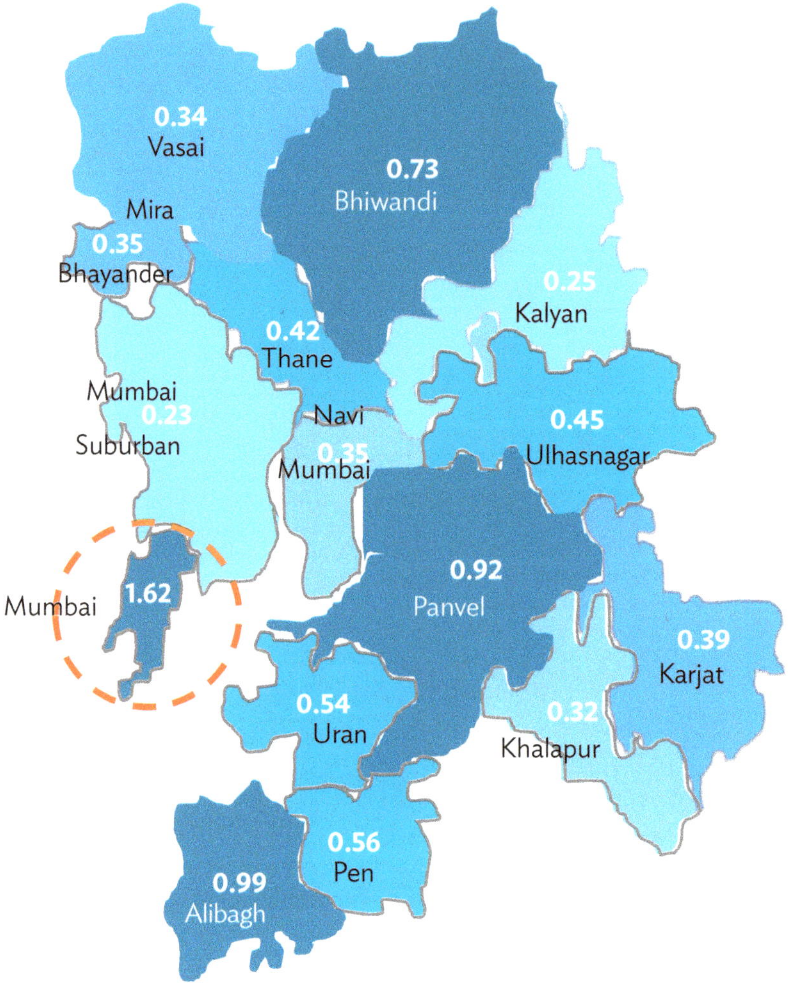

- 0.34 Vasai
- 0.73 Bhiwandi
- 0.35 Mira Bhayander
- 0.42 Thane
- 0.25 Kalyan
- 0.23 Mumbai Suburban
- 0.35 Navi Mumbai
- 0.45 Ulhasnagar
- 1.62 Mumbai
- 0.92 Panvel
- 0.39 Karjat
- 0.54 Uran
- 0.32 Khalapur
- 0.56 Pen
- 0.99 Alibagh

Data source: Mumbai Metropolitan Region Development Authority. 2003. *Population and Employment Profile of Mumbai Metropolitan Region*. Mumbai.

Figure 4: Current Modal Share of Public Transport in Mumbai

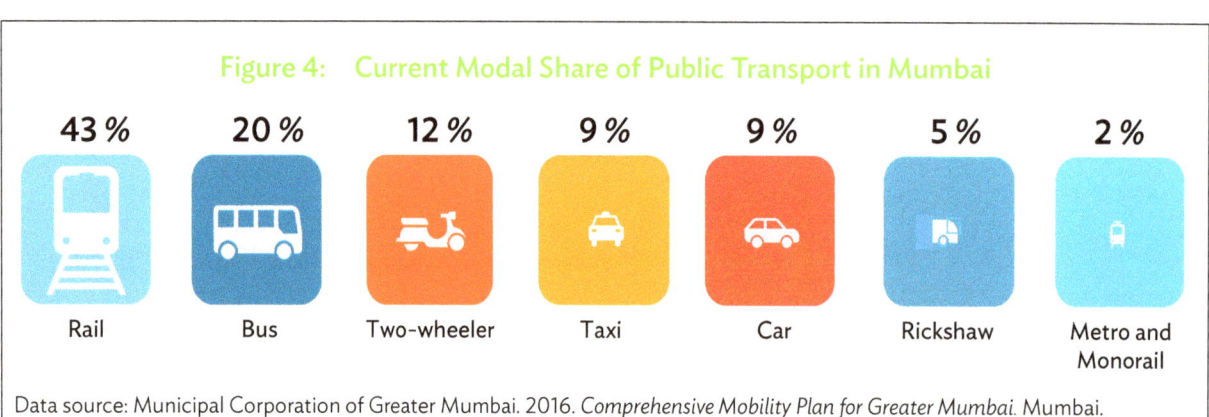

43%	20%	12%	9%	9%	5%	2%
Rail	Bus	Two-wheeler	Taxi	Car	Rickshaw	Metro and Monorail

Data source: Municipal Corporation of Greater Mumbai. 2016. *Comprehensive Mobility Plan for Greater Mumbai*. Mumbai.

Suburban rail is the lifeline of Mumbai and carries more than 7.5 million daily passengers on its almost 400 km network. It utilizes 258 trains to run more than 3,000 train services daily.[5] Passengers travel under extremely overcrowded "super dense crush load" conditions. The trains have a design capacity of 1,750 people (per 9-coach train), but are currently transporting roughly 5,000 people during periods of peak demand. This excessive jam-packing of people in the rail coaches (at more than 3 times the design capacity) indicates that there are 14 passengers per square meter crowded into the suburban trains, making it one of most overcrowded public transport systems in the world.

Highly crowded Mumbai suburban rail system. Overcrowding at suburban railway stations leads to unsafe conditions at the stations as well as while boarding and de-boarding the trains (photo by Cool Runnings India in *Flickr*).

Meanwhile, the bus system operated by the state-owned BEST caters to more than 3.5 million passengers daily, using its fleet of 4,336 buses. However, bus transportation in Mumbai occurs on highly congested roads. The number of private vehicles has increased from 2.3 million in 2005 to 7.2 million in 2017. This increase in private vehicles has further added to the already high congestion on the road network. As shown in Figure 5, the average vehicle speed on the roads of Mumbai (8.1 km/hour) is significantly less than the average speed of leading cities of the world. Further, the road congestion index for Mumbai is also significantly higher than the index of these leading cities.[6]

---

[5] Mumbai Railway Vikas Corporation Ltd. 2019. *Corporate Plan 2034*. Mumbai.
[6] A. Bhide. 2019. *Need of Metro for Sustainable Development*. A PowerPoint presentation for Mumbai Metro Rail Corporation Ltd. 20 September.

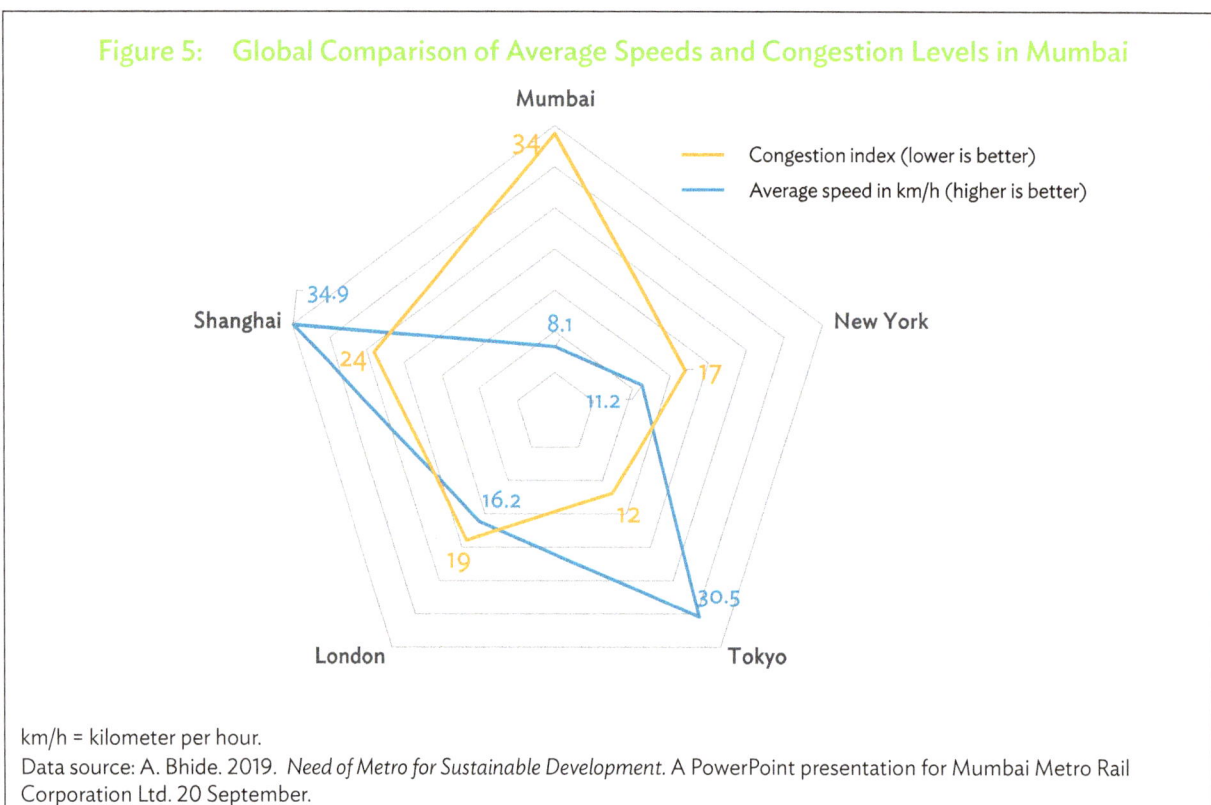

km/h = kilometer per hour.
Data source: A. Bhide. 2019. *Need of Metro for Sustainable Development.* A PowerPoint presentation for Mumbai Metro Rail Corporation Ltd. 20 September.

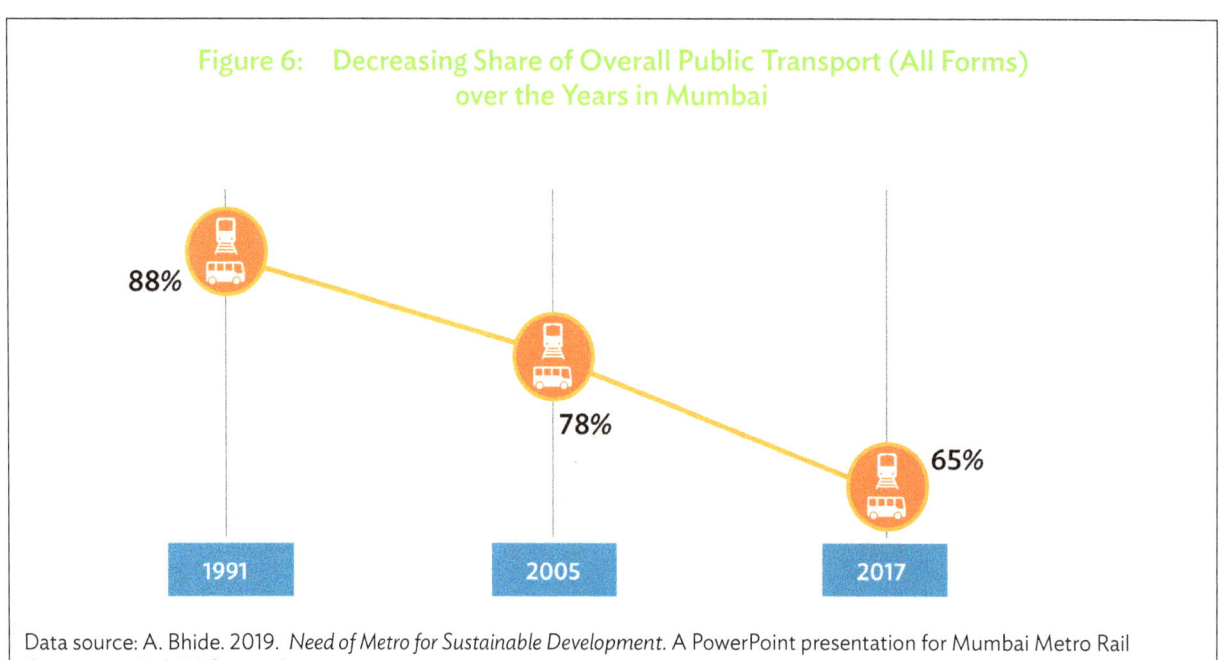

Data source: A. Bhide. 2019. *Need of Metro for Sustainable Development.* A PowerPoint presentation for Mumbai Metro Rail Corporation Ltd. 20 September.

Due to the reasons outlined, the overall share of public transport has been gradually decreasing over the last few decades in Mumbai. It has dropped from 88% in 1991 to 65% in 2017 (Figure 6).

The suburban rail system has already undertaken several capacity enhancements, such as reducing the headway on all lines by respacing the signaling, converting the overhead power supply system from direct current to alternating current, replacing 9-coach trains with 12-coach trains, extending the lengths of all platforms, etc. Several lines have already been doubled, tripled, and, in some cases, the fifth and sixth lines have been added (e.g., the Borivali–Virar section). The need for an extensive metro-based public transportation network in Mumbai becomes even more stark when the current metro coverage in Mumbai is compared with other cities across the world (Map 5).

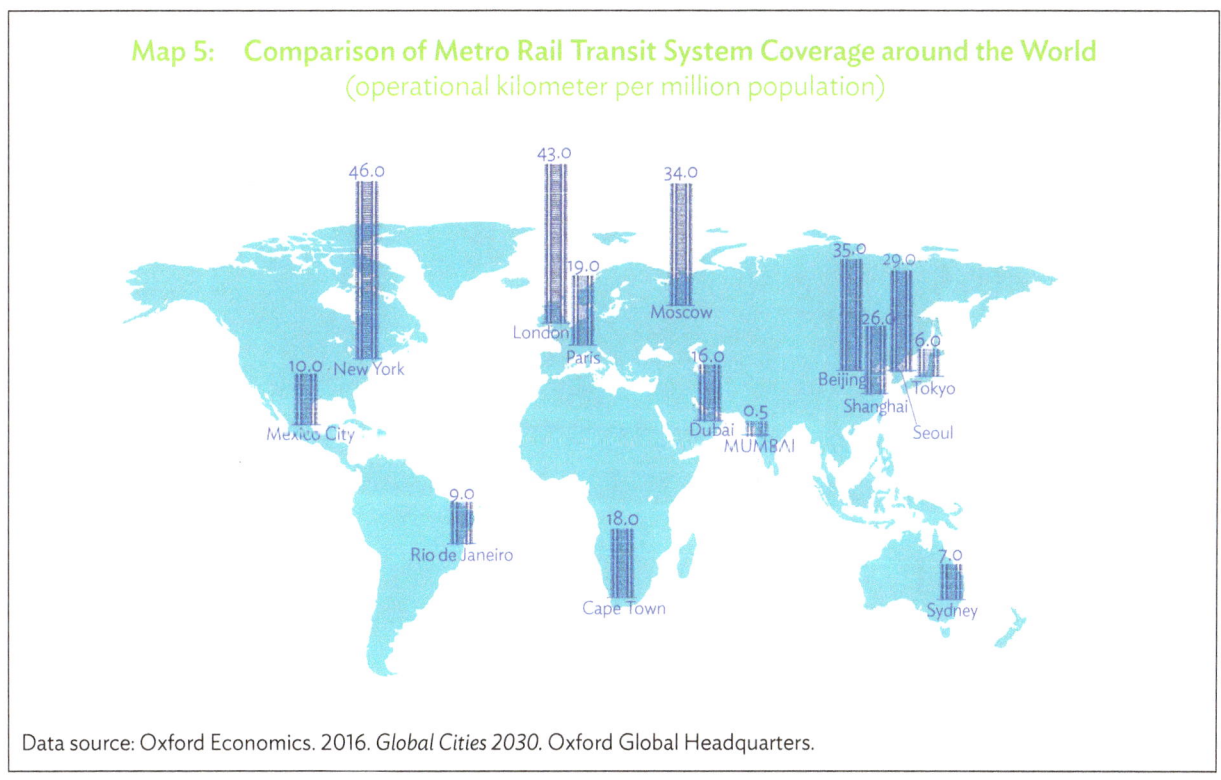

Map 5: Comparison of Metro Rail Transit System Coverage around the World (operational kilometer per million population)

Data source: Oxford Economics. 2016. *Global Cities 2030*. Oxford Global Headquarters.

As illustrated in Map 5, the operational metro length per million people in Mumbai is extremely low as compared with other global cities. Not only is this true with respect to developed cities such as New York, London, Paris, Dubai, and Sydney, but it is also significantly lower than developing cities such as Rio de Janeiro, Cape Town, and Moscow in the countries of Brazil, Russian Federation, India, People's Republic of China, and South Africa (BRICS).

The Mumbai Metro coverage of 0.5 km of length per million people is primarily due to the currently operational Line 1. This metric is expected to increase to 14.0 km of metro length per million people upon completion of construction of the Mumbai Metro Master Plan of 277 km of metro network.

If the Mumbai Metro Master Plan was not to be realized, the share of public transport in Mumbai will continue to fall. This would further lead to development challenges in the city as metro systems typically offer easier accessibility, cleaner environment, safer transit, and comfortable journeys to a huge number of people and help in inclusive socioeconomic development.

Train at a halt. Metro trains in Mumbai provide a safe, clean and efficient mode of transport (photo by V_E/Shutterstock.com).

Breathing New Life into the City

Mumbai Metro Master Plan

Mumbai has greatly benefited from the mature and robust Mumbai suburban railway. The suburban rail network is developed, operated, and maintained by Indian Railways and has transported the people of Mumbai for more than 150 years. The first suburban train was started in 1867 between Virar and Back Bay (near current-day Churchgate). Currently, the Mumbai region is served by two zones of the Indian Railways: Western Railway and Central Railway. The Western Railway line, going northward from Churchgate, runs parallel to the west coast of Mumbai; whereas, the Central Railway line, running from Chhatrapati Shivaji Terminus, serves central and eastern Mumbai (Map 6).

However, the rapid expansion and spatial growth of Mumbai has resulted in more and more people living further away from central Mumbai (where most of the jobs are located). As is evident from the average commuter

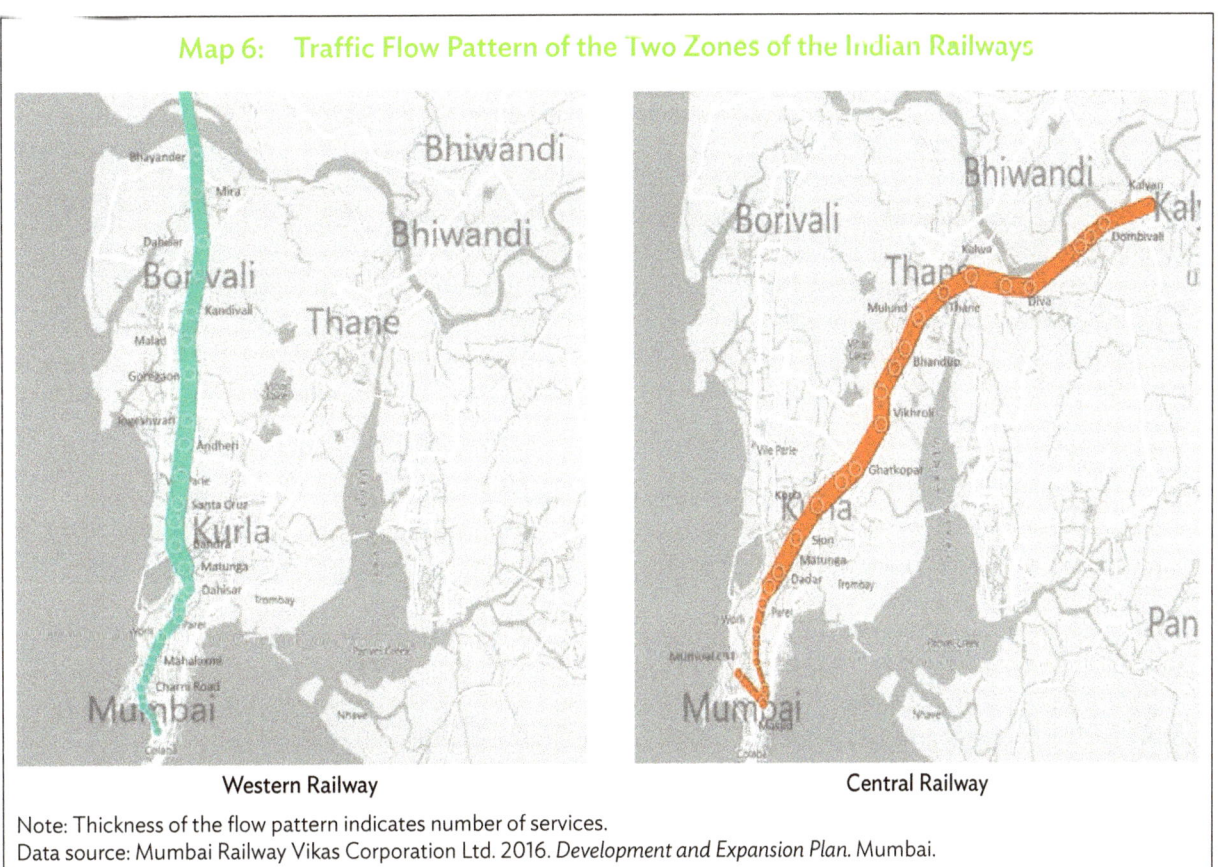

Map 6: Traffic Flow Pattern of the Two Zones of the Indian Railways

Note: Thickness of the flow pattern indicates number of services.
Data source: Mumbai Railway Vikas Corporation Ltd. 2016. *Development and Expansion Plan*. Mumbai.

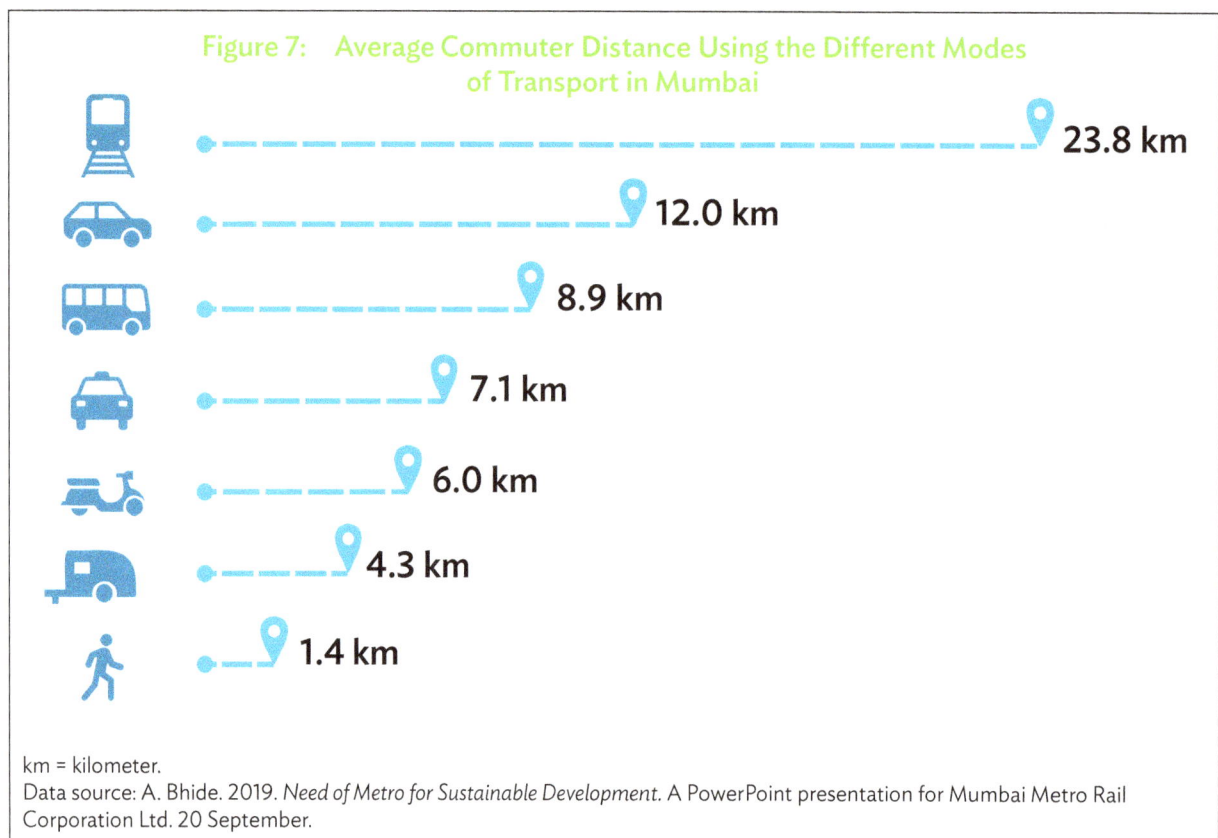

Figure 7: Average Commuter Distance Using the Different Modes of Transport in Mumbai

23.8 km
12.0 km
8.9 km
7.1 km
6.0 km
4.3 km
1.4 km

km = kilometer.
Data source: A. Bhide. 2019. *Need of Metro for Sustainable Development*. A PowerPoint presentation for Mumbai Metro Rail Corporation Ltd. 20 September.

distance of various modes of transport in Mumbai, people living further away from central Mumbai prefer the suburban railways to commute daily between home and work. The average distance travelled by commuters in the suburban railways is highest at 23.8 km per trip (Figure 7).

As discussed previously, the current public transportation systems, including the suburban railway and the Brihanmumbai Electricity Supply and Transport (BEST) buses, are under extreme pressure in terms of capacity and quality. To resolve the existing transport infrastructure challenges, as well as to improve the regional connectivity to meet the city's future needs, the Government of Maharashtra and the Mumbai Metropolitan Region Development Authority (MMRDA) prepared the Master Plan for the Mumbai Metro in 2004. The original Master Plan included nine corridors covering 146.5 km. The Master Plan has been updated to include a total of 12 lines covering a length of 277 km (Map 7).

The Mumbai Metro Master Plan is expected to not only increase public transport modal share in the Mumbai Metropolitan Region (MMR), but also improve the quality of life, convenience of transportation, safety of commuting, and accessibility for all socioeconomic groups (specifically the poor, women, and children).

The Mumbai Metro Master Plan will serve six business districts (Cuffe Parade, Fort, Lower Parel, Nariman Point, Santacruz Electronics Export Processing Zone, and Worli), in addition to providing connectivity to Chhatrapati Shivaji Maharaj International Airport and Navi Mumbai International Airport. Importantly, the Mumbai Metro Master Plan will help in connecting areas that are not currently served by the suburban rail network.

Another key aspect of the Mumbai Metro Master Plan will be the additional mobility options for travelling along the East–West corridors. Lines 1 and 6 will provide East–West connectivity in Greater Mumbai, while Line 8 will

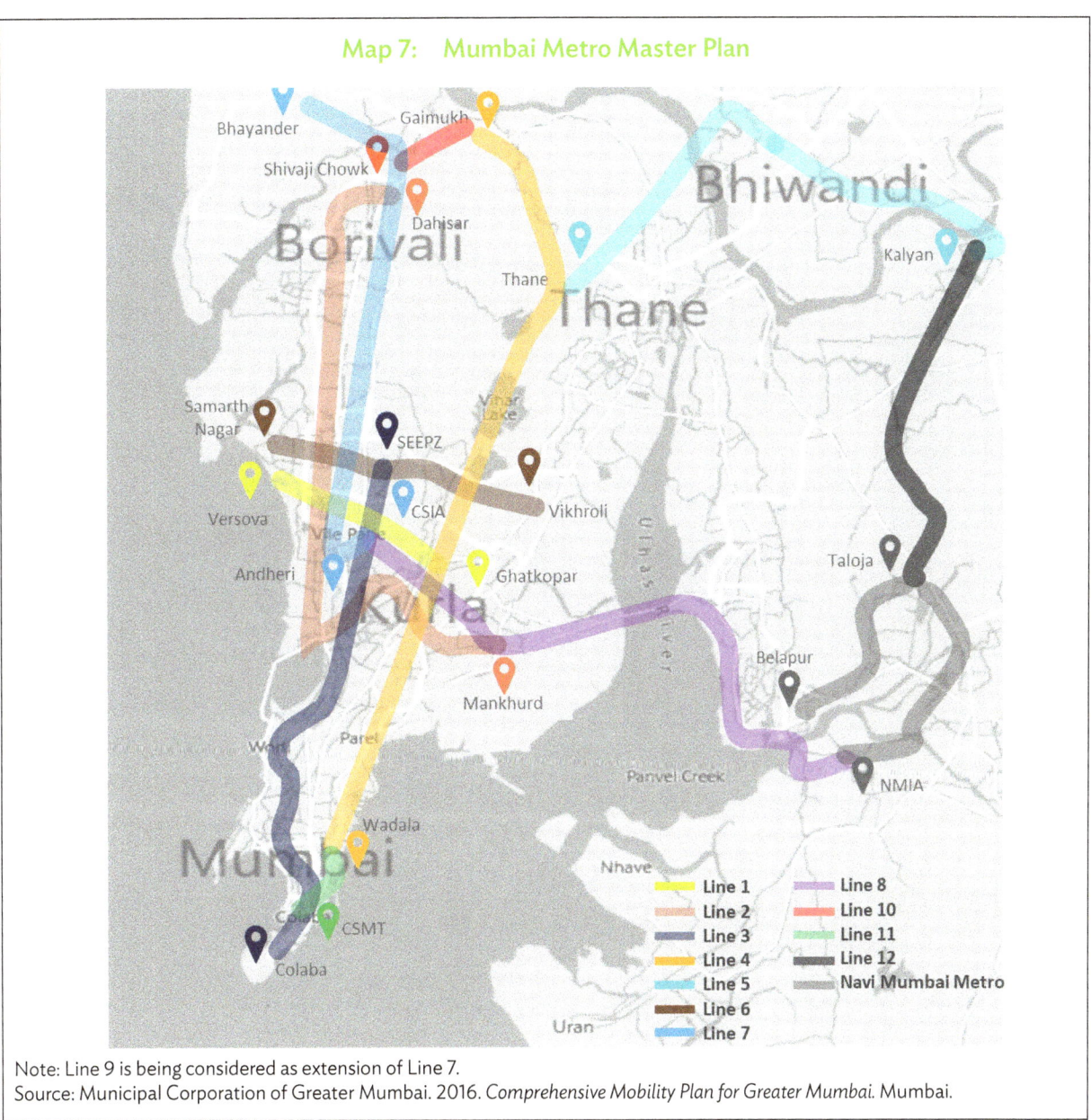

Map 7: Mumbai Metro Master Plan

Note: Line 9 is being considered as extension of Line 7.
Source: Municipal Corporation of Greater Mumbai. 2016. *Comprehensive Mobility Plan for Greater Mumbai*. Mumbai.

connect Mumbai with Navi Mumbai. Further, Line 12 will connect with the Navi Mumbai Metro lines. The key characteristics of each metro line in the Master Plan have been summarized in Figure 8.

On 26 February 2019, the Asian Development Bank (ADB) approved a $926 million loan for the Mumbai Metro.[7] The loan will support Lines 2A, 2B, and 7 (covering a total distance of about 58 km), where ADB will assist the MMRDA in financing the procurement of rolling stock, signaling and train control systems, as well as station access, platform systems, and multimodal integration. Lines 2A, 2B, and 7 are expected to cater to almost 2 million commuters per day, after the operations stabilize. The ADB loan can greatly benefit these metro lines,

---

[7] ADB. 2019. *Report and Recommendation of the President to the Board of Directors: Proposed Loan to India for the Mumbai Metro Rail Systems Project.* Manila.

Figure 8: Details of the Mumbai Metro Master Plan

	Length (km)	No. of stations	Cost (₹million)	Owner	Debt Funding Agency
Line 1	11	12	23,560	MMRDA	
Line 2	42	38	173,960	MMRDA	ADB
Line 3	34	27	231,360	MMRC	JICA
Line 4	35	34	145,490	MMRDA	KfW
Line 5	25	17	84,170	MMRDA	AIIB
Line 6	15	13	65,160	MMRDA	NDB
Line 7	16	13	62,080	MMRDA	ADB
Line 8	35	To be finalized	150,000	MMRDA	To be finalized
Line 10	9	4	44,760	MMRDA	To be finalized
Line 11	12	10	87,390	MMRDA	To be finalized
Line 12	21	17	58,650	MMRDA	To be finalized

₹ = Indian rupee, ADB = Asian Development Bank, AIIB = Asian Infrastructure Investment Bank, JICA = Japan International Cooperation Agency, KfW = Kreditanstalt für Wiederaufbau (German development cooperation), km = kilometer, MMRDA = Mumbai Metropolitan Region Development Authority.
Note: Line 9 is being considered as extension of Line 7.
Data source: Mumbai Metropolitan Region Development Authority.

which are expected to improve transport safety and comfort for the people, especially the poor and vulnerable. These metro lines are also expected to provide enhanced access to economic opportunities and social services for all socioeconomic groups in Mumbai

The ADB loan will be used for the following aspects:
- design, manufacture, testing, and maintenance of 378 energy-efficient rolling stock carriages;
- procurement, installation, and testing of an advanced signaling, train control, and platform access system for 58 km of metro lines; and
- establishment of a Mumbai Metro operations organization.

The ownership of the MMRDA and the Mumbai Metro Rail Corporation Limited and the financial assistance from agencies like ADB, Asian Infrastructure Investment Bank, Japan International Cooperation Agency, among others, have helped in the evolution of the respective metro lines (Figure 9).

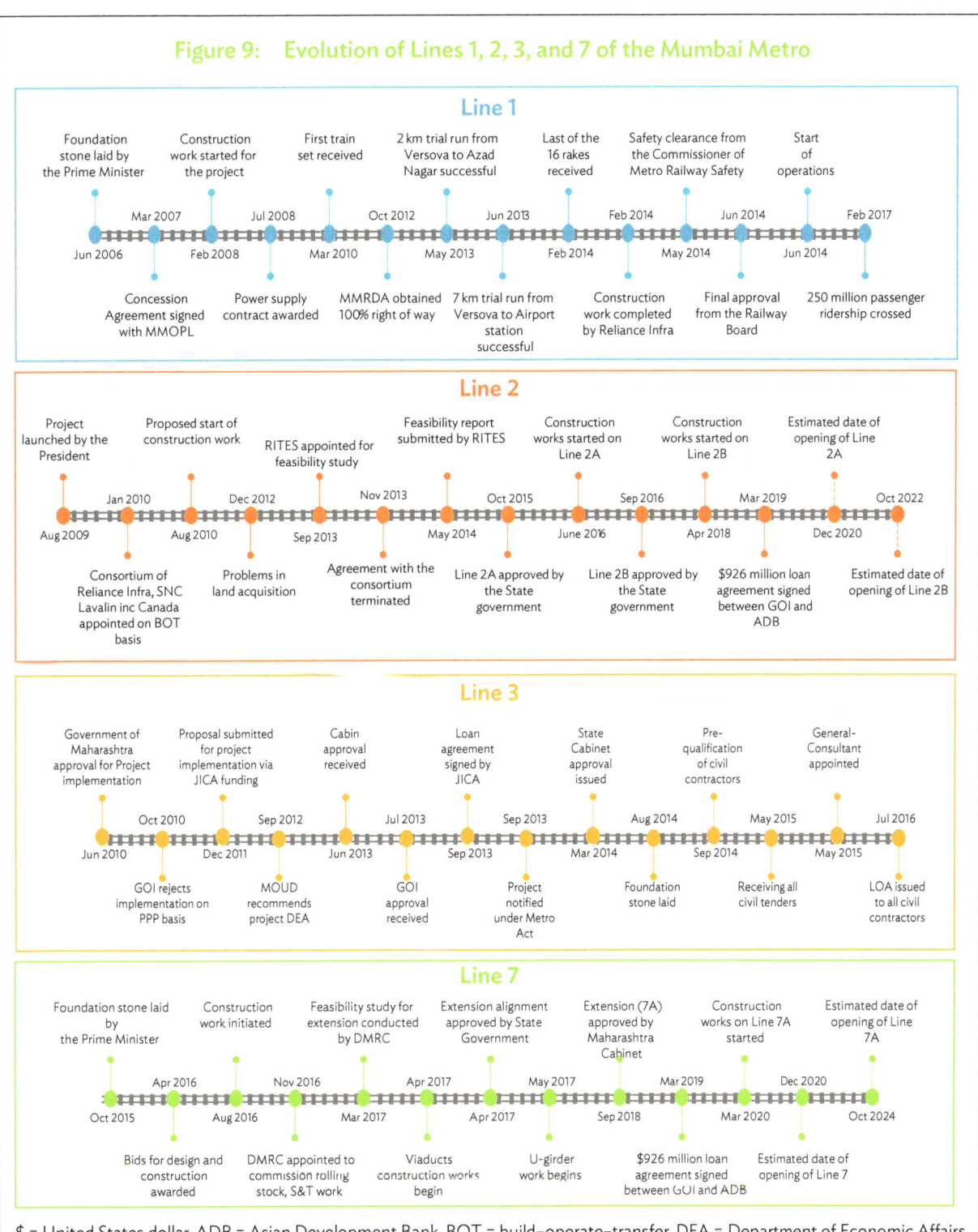

Figure 9: Evolution of Lines 1, 2, 3, and 7 of the Mumbai Metro

$ = United States dollar, ADB = Asian Development Bank, BOT = build–operate–transfer, DEA = Department of Economic Affairs, DMRC = Delhi Metro Rail Corporation, GOI = Government of India, JICA = Japan International Cooperation Agency, km = kilometer; MMOPL = Mumbai Metro One Private Limited, MMRDA = Mumbai Metropolitan Region Development Authority, MOUD = Ministry of Urban Development, PPP = public–private partnership, RITES = Rail India Technical and Economic Service, S&T = signaling and telecommunication.
Data source: Mumbai Metropolitan Region Development Authority.

Project Progress

The realization of the Mumbai Metro Master Plan is a complex task that is being managed by the MMRDA and by Mumbai Metro Rail Corporation Limited for Line 3. It consists of constructing several lines, which in turn include several packages and phases. The foundation stone for the first phase of the Mumbai Metro project was laid in 2006, and the construction work began in 2008.

All lines of the Mumbai Metro Master Plan are expected to be completed by the year 2026 (Figure 10).

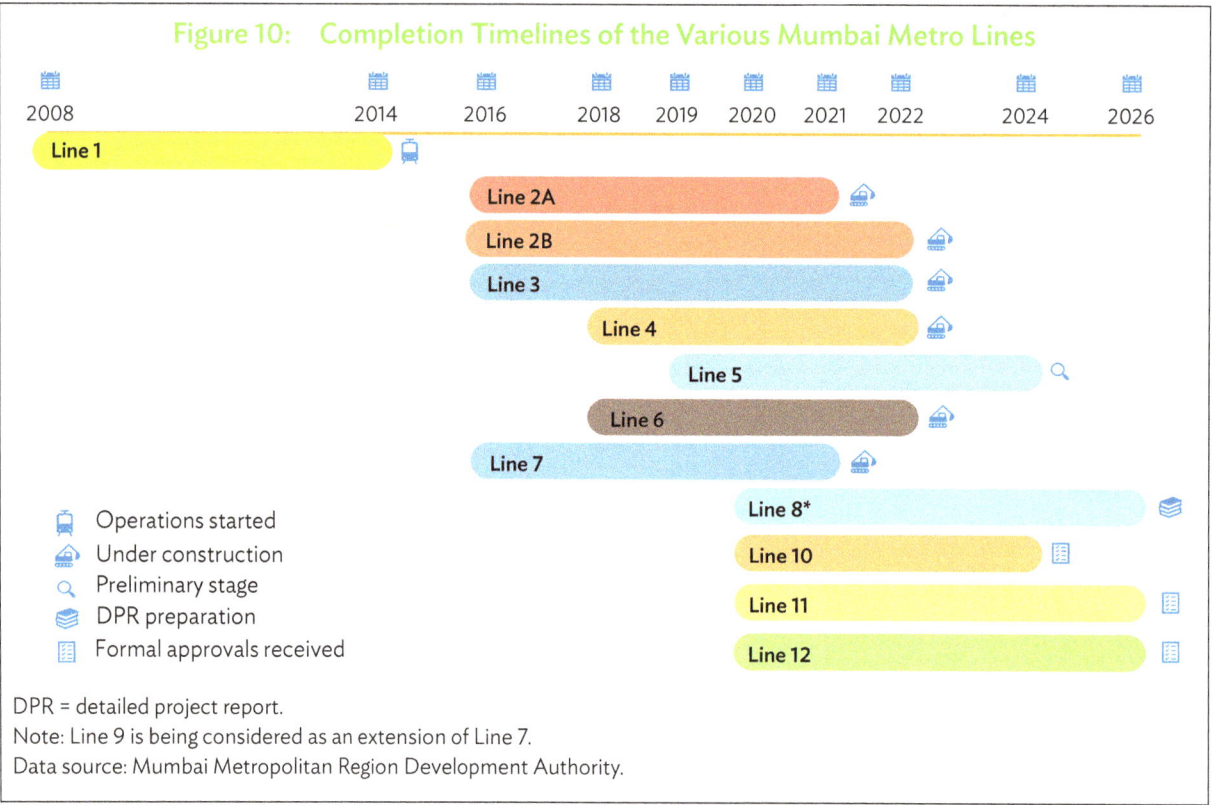

Figure 10: Completion Timelines of the Various Mumbai Metro Lines

DPR = detailed project report.
Note: Line 9 is being considered as an extension of Line 7.
Data source: Mumbai Metropolitan Region Development Authority.

As seen in Figure 10, Line 1 has been operational since June 2014, and Lines 2A, 2B, 3, 4, 6, and 7 are currently at different stages of construction. Line 8 is in the detailed project report preparation stage, while Line 5 is at the preliminary stage (alignment finalization). Lines 10, 11, and 12 have all received formal approvals for proceeding as well. Meanwhile, Line 9 is not shown separately in illustrations of the Mumbai Metro Lines as it is being considered as an extension of Line 7.

The key to unlock the total value from the Mumbai Metro Master Plan will be its on-time construction completion in the short to medium term. Lines 2A and 7 are expected to be operational by 2021, and the construction works have reached their last stages.

Construction works for Line 2A (top photo) and Line 7 (bottom photo). Lines 2A and 7 are targeted to start operations by 2021 (photos by Mumbai Metropolitan Region Development Authority).

Income inequality in Mumbai. Slums of Mumbai against the backdrop of Mumbai's skyscrapers highlight the income inequality in the city (photo by M. H. Ameeq in *Pixabay*

Contributing toward an Equitable City

Income Inequality in our Society—A Global and National Perspective

The Gini coefficient is a well-established statistical index to measure the disparity of income between the rich and the poor. It is used for determining the income inequality within nations as well as within states. Its value ranges between 0 and 1, with 0 indicating *perfect equality* and 1 indicating *perfect inequality*. Thus, a high Gini coefficient indicates high socioeconomic disparity in the society due to high differences in income distribution.

To understand the extent of income inequality in India on a global level, datasets from the World Bank and Central Intelligence Agency factbook (having data pertaining to more than 150 countries) were analyzed. As can be seen in Figure 11, the majority of countries fall within the small economies segment (with a GDP of less than

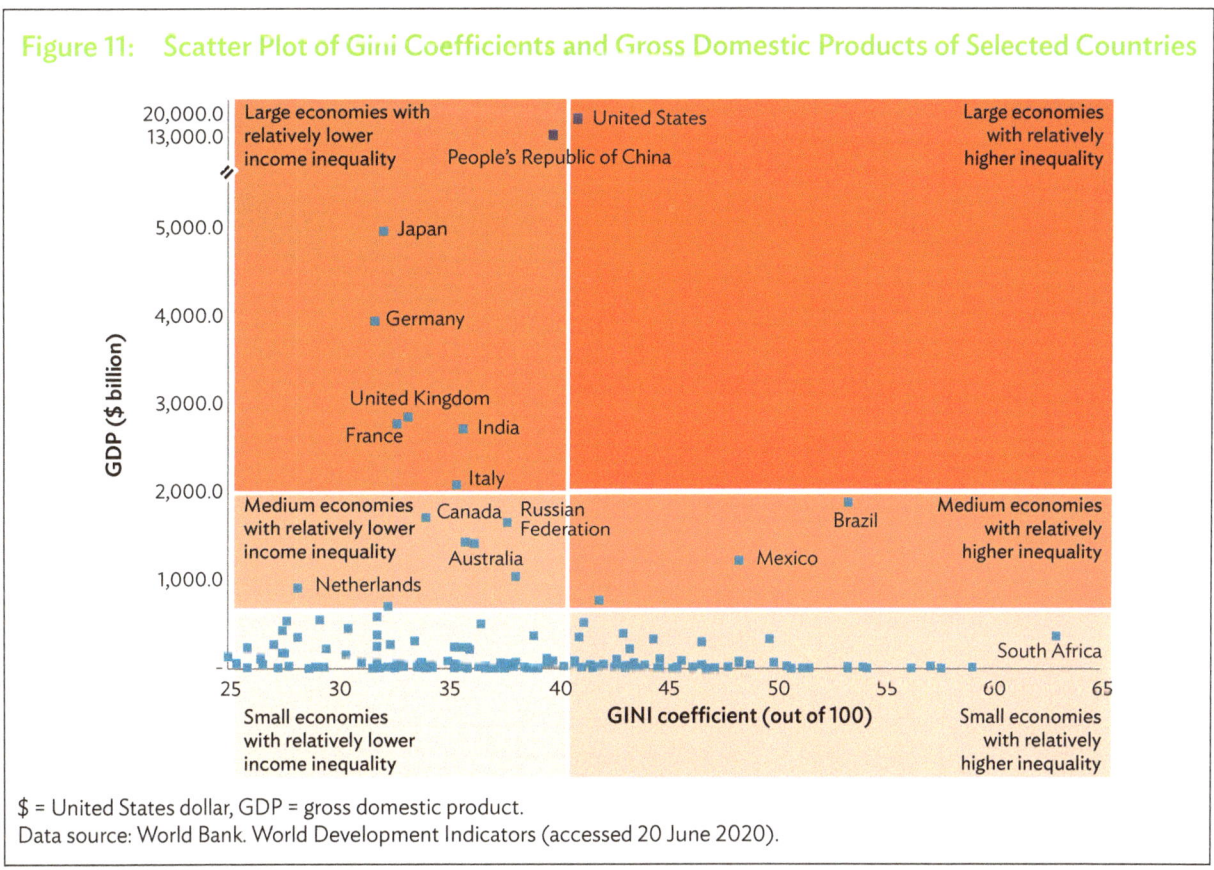

Figure 11: Scatter Plot of Gini Coefficients and Gross Domestic Products of Selected Countries

$ = United States dollar, GDP = gross domestic product.
Data source: World Bank. World Development Indicators (accessed 20 June 2020).

$0.5 trillion). These smaller economies have an almost even split on either side, with a Gini coefficient of 0.40 (which is the mean of the Gini coefficients of all countries). India lies in the segment that can be classified as a large economy (having a GDP of more than $2 trillion), with a relatively lower Gini coefficient (0.37). However, most of the developed countries like Germany, Japan, France, and the United Kingdom have Gini coefficients less than India, while still generating similar or higher economic output. Further, the Gini coefficients of the highest GDP countries in the world, i.e., the United States and the People's Republic of China, are only marginally higher than that of India.[8] Hence, India needs to further bridge its socioeconomic gap to be at par with the leading countries of the world.

A deeper understanding of income inequality in India can be gathered by assessing the state-wise Gini coefficients (Map 8). An analysis of the Planning Commission of India's dataset of state-wise Gini coefficients indicates the major states where income inequality is higher. Maharashtra's Gini coefficient (0.38) is the fourth highest among all states and Union Territories in India. Further, its Gini coefficient is higher than the overall Gini coefficient of India (0.37).[9] Thus, there is considerable opportunity for interventions that can bridge income inequality and the subsequent socioeconomic disparity in Maharashtra.

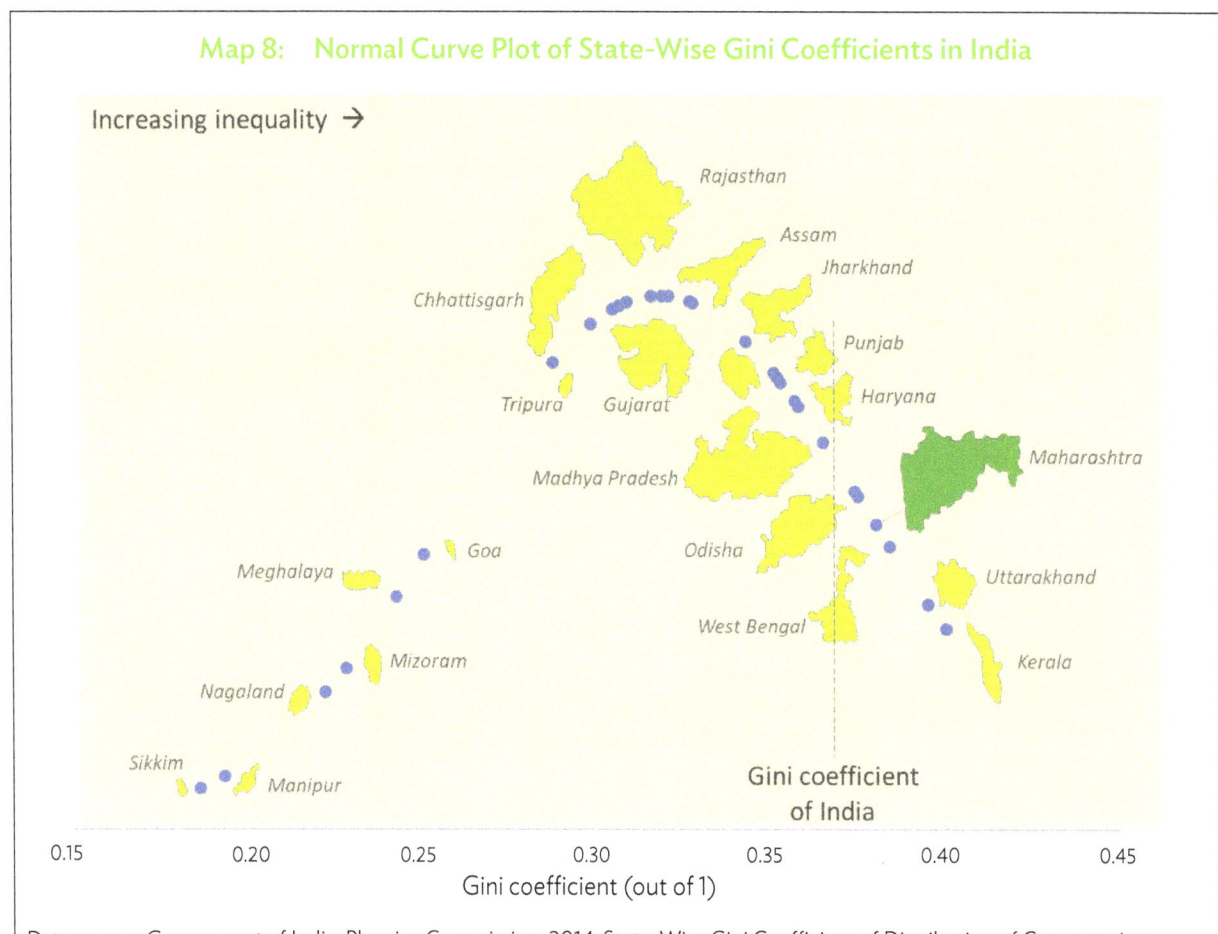

Map 8: Normal Curve Plot of State-Wise Gini Coefficients in India

Data source: Government of India, Planning Commission. 2014. State-Wise Gini Coefficient of Distribution of Consumption: 1973–1974 to 2009–2010. *Databook for Use of Deputy Chairman, Planning Commission.* 10 March. p. 100.

---

[8] World Bank. World Development Indicators (accessed 20 June 2020).
[9] Government of India, Planning Commission. 2014. State-Wise Gini Coefficient of Distribution of Consumption: 1973–1974 to 2009–2010. *Databook for Use of Deputy Chairman, Planning Commission.* 10 March. p. 100.

Since the Mumbai Metropolitan Region (MMR) is the biggest contributor to the GDP of Maharashtra, interventions in the MMR can have substantial impact on improving the socioeconomic disparity in Maharashtra and, hence, in India.

Existing Socioeconomic Profile of the Mumbai Metropolitan Region

The MMR is the second largest metropolitan city in India (after Delhi), and the 11th largest metropolitan city in the world. To make the MMR more equitable, it is crucial to identify the vulnerable groups that need socioeconomic upliftment. The target groups that need specific attention, due to limited availability as well as accessibility to opportunities, are low-income workers, women, and the differently abled. Figure 12 presents some important socioeconomic indexes for these groups.

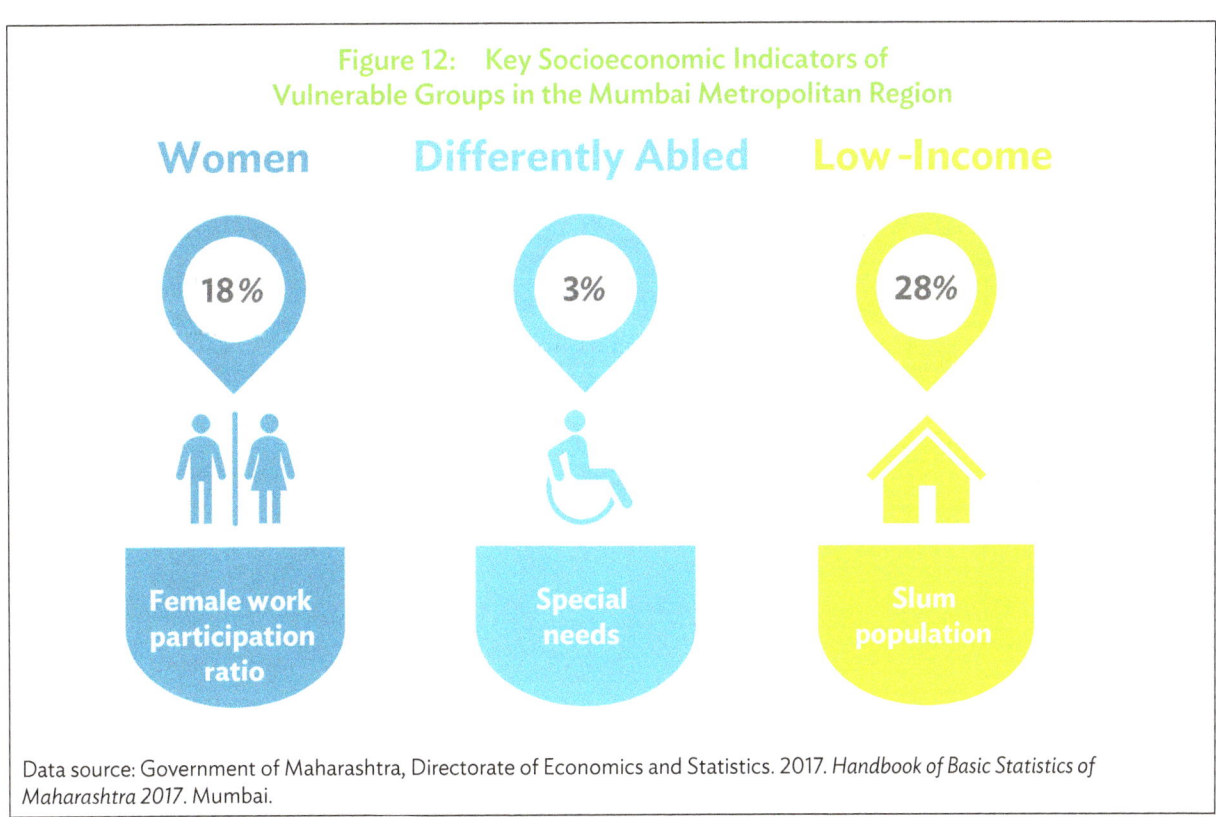

Figure 12: Key Socioeconomic Indicators of Vulnerable Groups in the Mumbai Metropolitan Region

Data source: Government of Maharashtra, Directorate of Economics and Statistics. 2017. *Handbook of Basic Statistics of Maharashtra 2017*. Mumbai.

From a gender point of view, the MMR's sex ratio (859 females per 1,000 males) is skewed toward males. This is lower than the sex ratios of India (906 females per 1,000 males) and Maharashtra (896 females per 1,000 males). This gender imbalance is further apparent at the work participation level (female work participation percentage of 18%, against a male work participation of almost 40%). Lack of comfortable transport options is a constant limitation to women's employment, education, and other activities. Ensuring an accessible public transport system for women can help to increase their participation in the work force.

Commuting in Mumbai's overcrowded trains. Women in saris commute with their children in overcrowded ladies' compartments of the Mumbai suburban trains (photo by Erin in *Flickr*).

From a special needs point of view, 3% of the MMR population is differently abled.[10] The lack of escalators, elevators, accessibility ramps, and platform-level boarding makes commuting difficult for this group and, hence, limits their development and opportunities. From an income point of view, 28% of the population in the MMR lives in slum areas. These people living on extremely low incomes cannot afford to dedicate income to safe and high-quality daily commuting and, hence, have limited access to growth opportunities. Thus, there is a need to empower the people in the low-income areas with high-quality and affordable commuting options.

Map 9 shows the major slum clusters where 28% of Mumbai's population lives. Dharavi, one of Asia's largest slums, is currently not served by the Mumbai suburban rail. However, Line 3 of the Mumbai Metro will have a dedicated station at Dharavi. This direct connectivity will enable easy accessibility to schools, hospitals, offices, etc., for the people in Dharavi.

---

[10] Government of Maharashtra, Directorate of Economics and Statistics. 2017. *Handbook of Basic Statistics of Maharashtra 2017*. Mumbai.

Contributing toward an Equitable City   25

A slum neighborhood in Dharavi, Mumbai. Slum clusters are common in Mumbai, and such slums form the livelihood of several people in the city (photo by Kounosu in *Wikimedia Commons*).

Map 9: Slum Clusters in Greater Mumbai

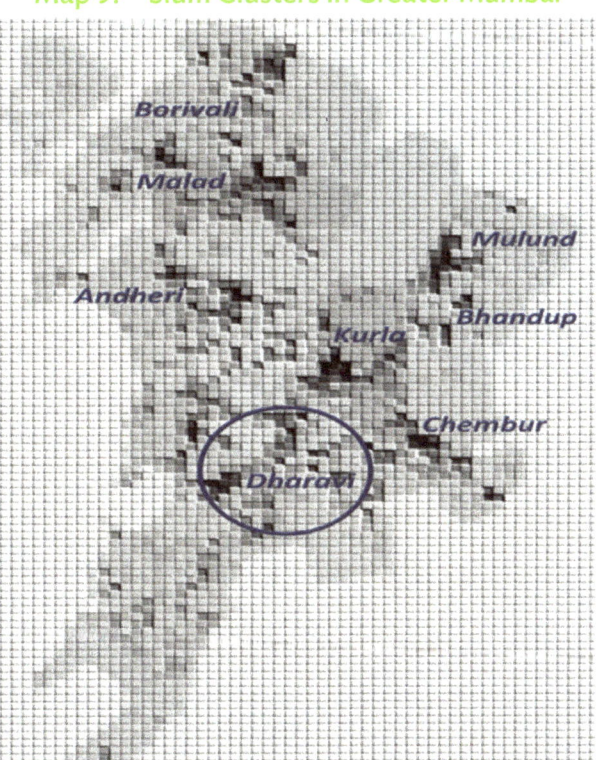

Data source: Government of India, Slum Rehabilitation Authority. 2016. *Ward and Village-Wise Slum Cluster Map of Greater Mumbai showing Area Boundaries of Competent Authority—GPS Survey 2015–2016*. Mumbai.

It is important here to also understand the existing profile of employment-generating sectors in the MMR. Figure 13 highlights the major sectors that provide employment. Providing better connectivity to these centers of employment can improve the quality of life of the people in the MMR.

As can be noted, the majority (71%) of employment in the MMR is generated by the tertiary sector, with most of this employment located within Mumbai City. Sectors like retail, hotels and restaurants, public administration, real estate, health, and education provide most of this employment, with the retail sector being the biggest provider. The secondary sector contributes 28% to the total MMR employment, almost all of which comes from manufacturing. Finally, the primary sector (comprising agriculture, mining, and fishing) accounts for only 1% of total employment. Hence, almost the entire population of Mumbai depends on business or manufacturing jobs.

To make the MMR truly equitable, more steps need to be taken to facilitate accessibility of the vulnerable groups to education, health care, housing, and employment. This is expected to result in an overall improvement in the socioeconomic indicators of the MMR.

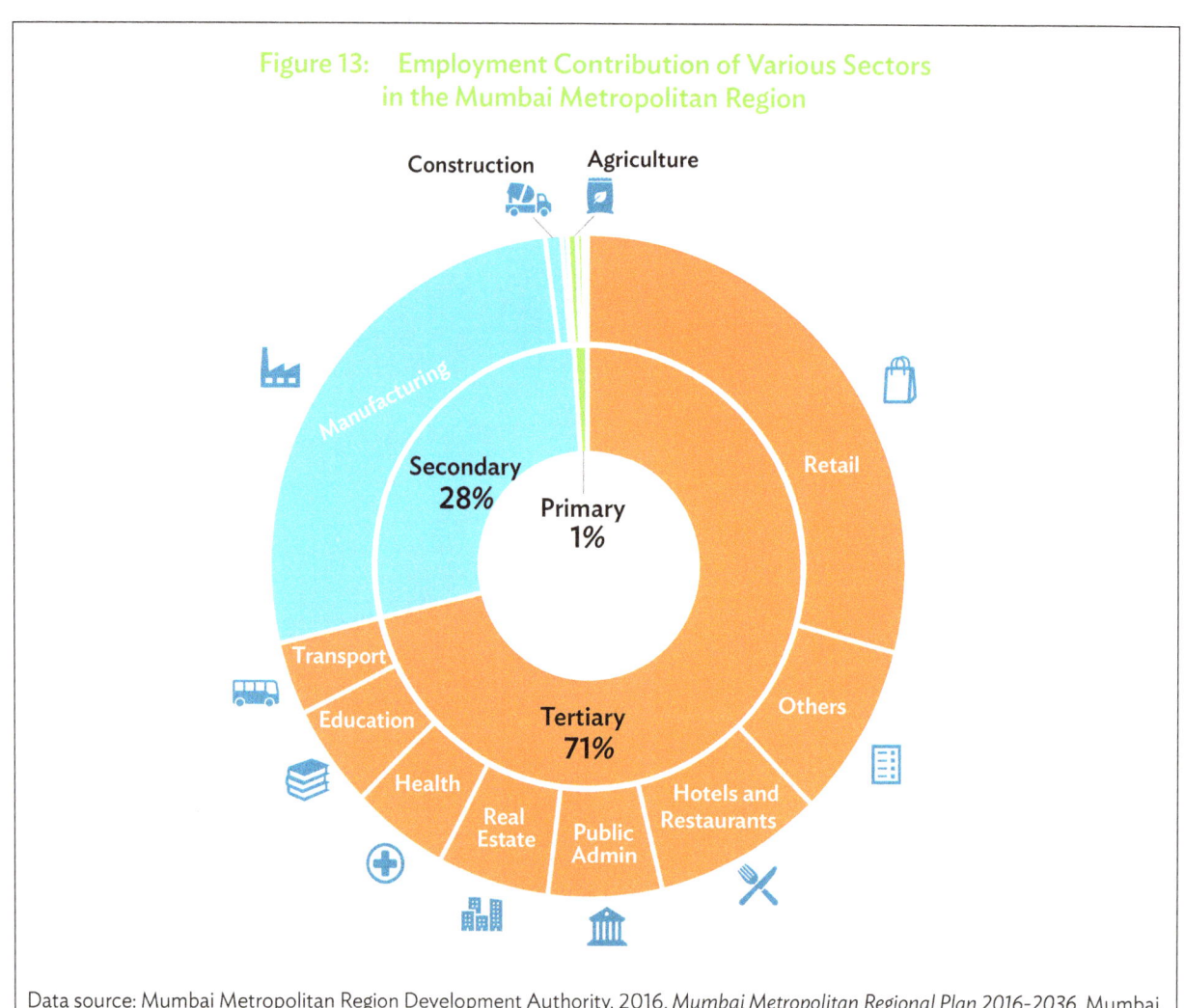

Figure 13: Employment Contribution of Various Sectors in the Mumbai Metropolitan Region

Data source: Mumbai Metropolitan Region Development Authority. 2016. *Mumbai Metropolitan Regional Plan 2016-2036*. Mumbai.

Projected Changes in the Profile of the Mumbai Metropolitan Region

Infrastructure in the MMR has always been under pressure due to the continuous influx of people. This influx has resulted in a gradual outward shift of the population away from the core of Mumbai. Since 1971, the population distribution in the Municipal Corporation of Greater Mumbai has decreased from 78% to 49%. This population distribution is further expected to decrease to 31% by 2041. Consequently, the population in surrounding areas (like Thane) is expected to increase to 49% by 2041 (up from 12% in 1971) (footnote 2). These changes in the land utilization have been captured in Figure 14 and will continue to shape the socioeconomic profile of the MMR.

The mushrooming of new urban areas (in orange) as well as new industrial areas (in red) on the right side of Figure 14 indicates the new centers for housing, as well as employment, that will be created outside the confines of Greater Mumbai. These will occur in addition to the increased usage intensity of the existing urban and industrial centers.

The major categories for employment in Mumbai are the business sector followed by the secondary sector. Hence, the above projected changes in land use patterns of urban and industrial areas, along with the projected changes in employment opportunities in the business and secondary sector, will play an important role in the future state of income equality in the MMR.

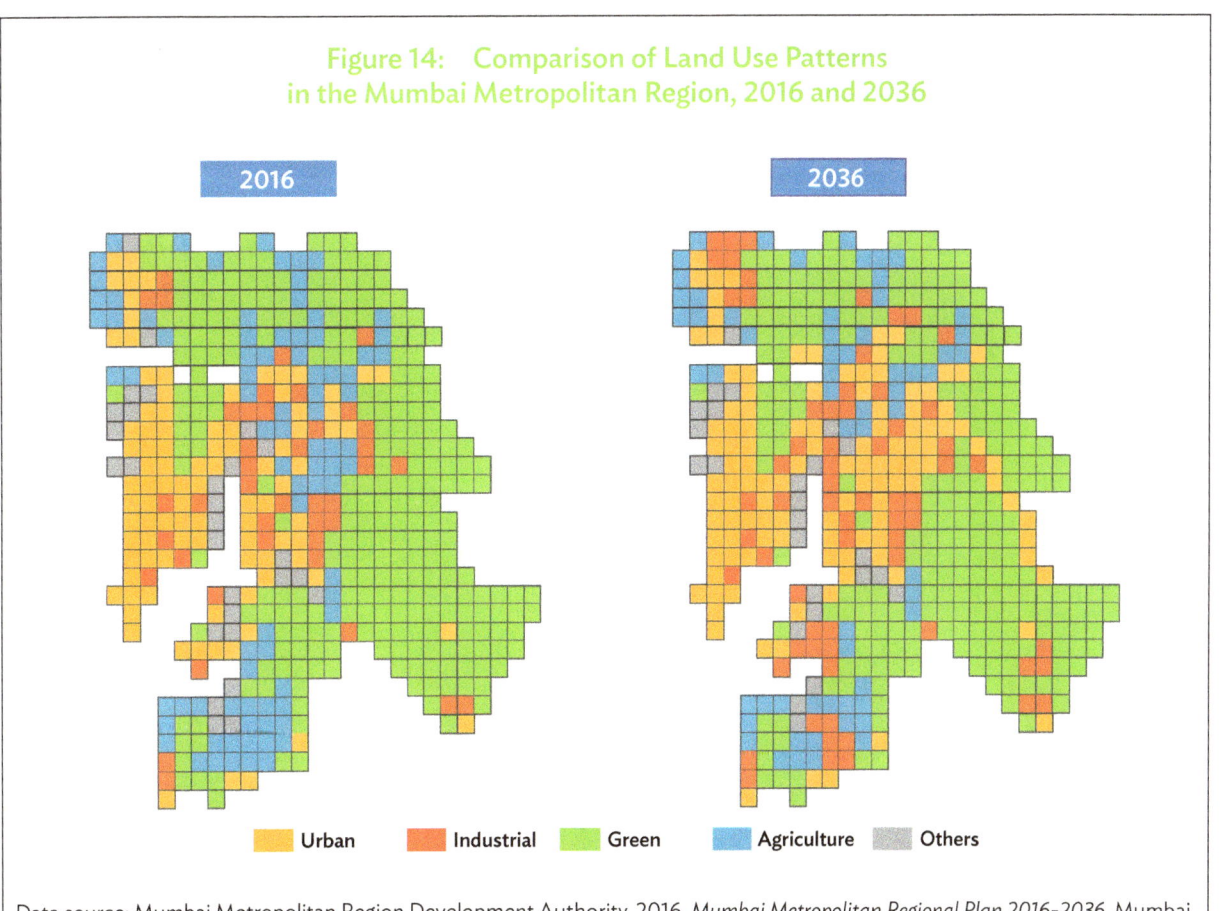

Figure 14: Comparison of Land Use Patterns in the Mumbai Metropolitan Region, 2016 and 2036

Data source: Mumbai Metropolitan Region Development Authority. 2016. *Mumbai Metropolitan Regional Plan 2016-2036*. Mumbai.

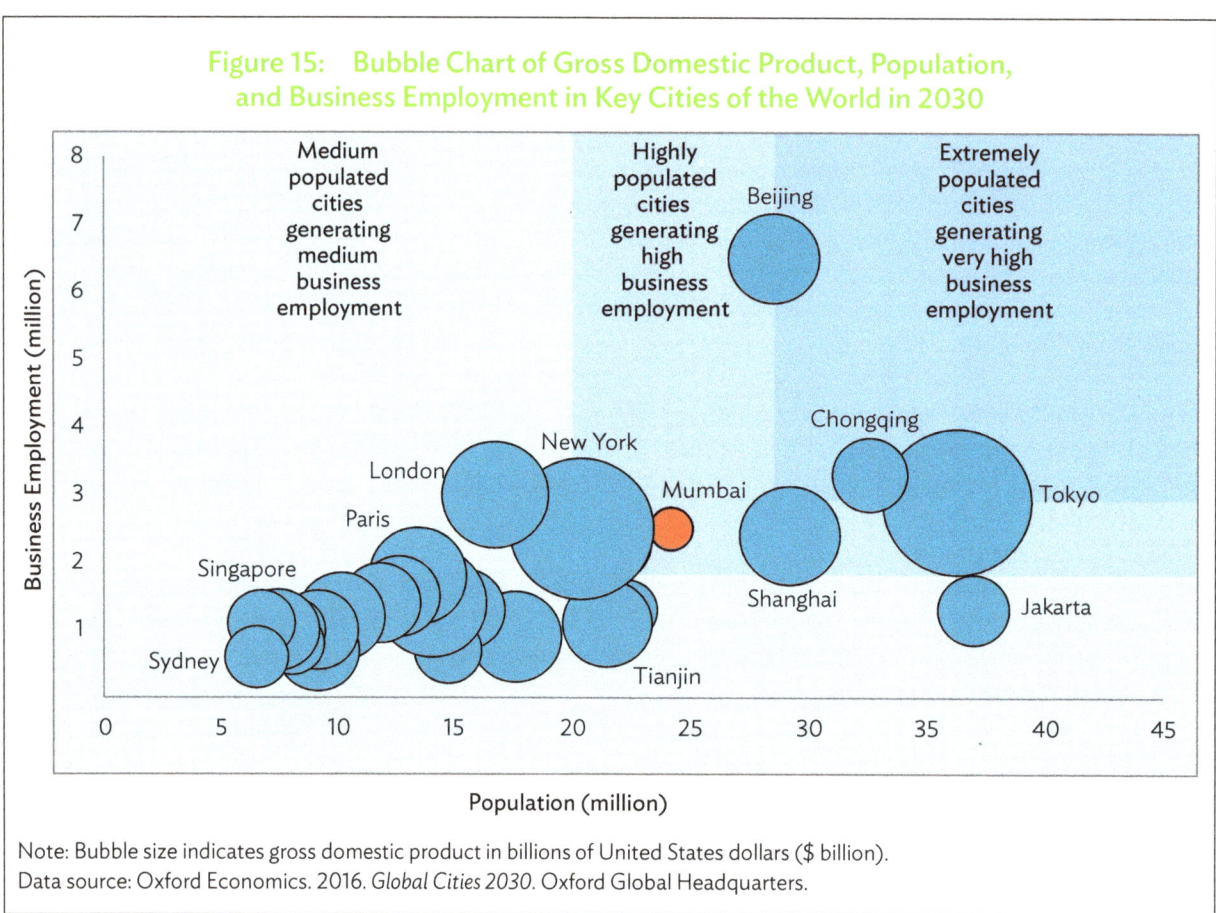

Figure 15: Bubble Chart of Gross Domestic Product, Population, and Business Employment in Key Cities of the World in 2030

Note: Bubble size indicates gross domestic product in billions of United States dollars ($ billion).
Data source: Oxford Economics. 2016. *Global Cities 2030*. Oxford Global Headquarters.

An analysis of the Oxford Economics data shows that, in 2030, Mumbai will continue its trajectory of growth in population, as well as in business-related employment (Figure 15). In fact, the MMR will be ranked fifth in the world in terms of business employment (2.5 million jobs) by 2030. With its increasing population that will contribute to the economic output of the city, the MMR will need a future-ready public transport system that empowers its citizens with access to existing and new centers of jobs.

Data also indicate that the MMR will be ranked 10th in the world in terms of secondary employment (2.9 million jobs) by 2030 (Figure 16).[11] This population will also need a future-ready public transport system that provides accessibility to the centers of secondary jobs.

---

[11] Oxford Economics. 2016. *Global Cities 2030*. Oxford Global Headquarters.

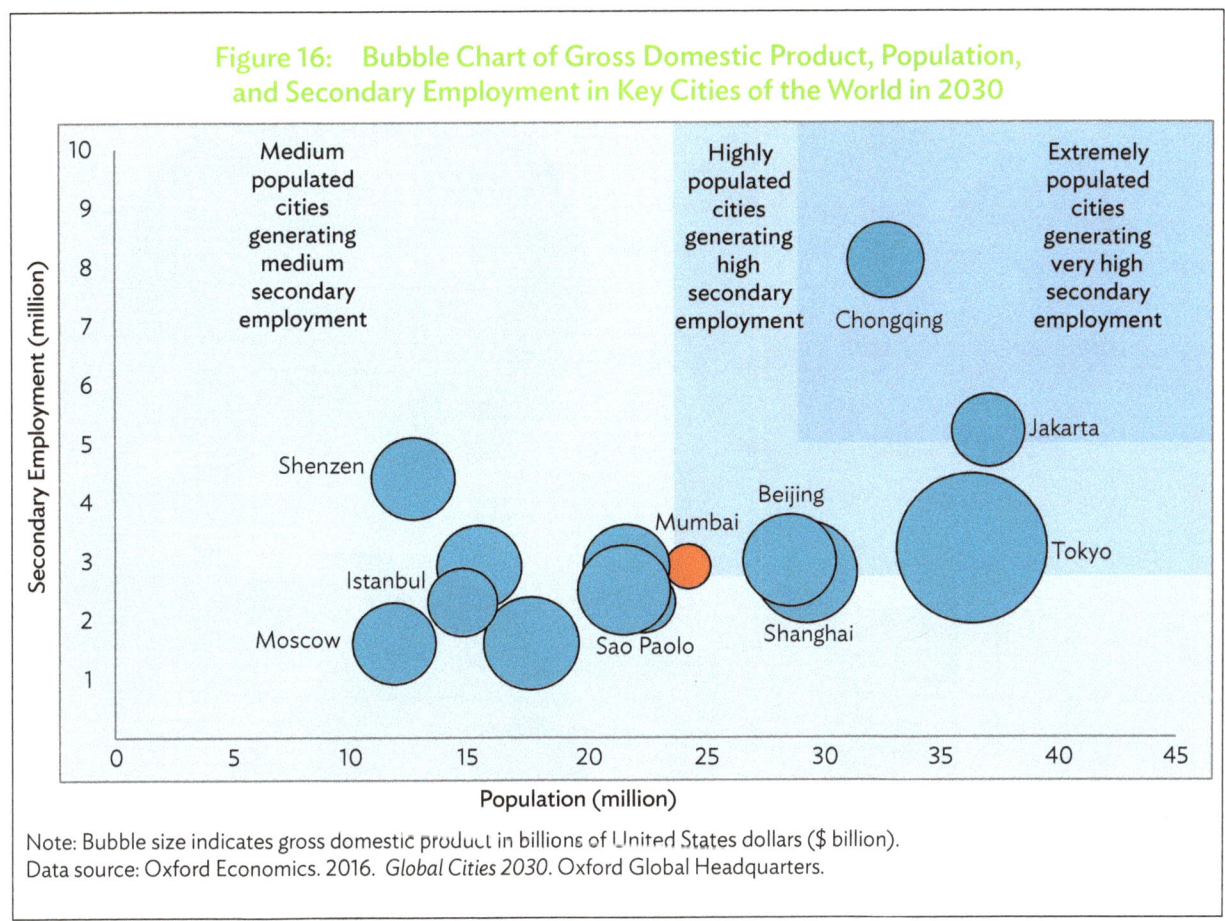

Figure 16: Bubble Chart of Gross Domestic Product, Population, and Secondary Employment in Key Cities of the World in 2030

Note: Bubble size indicates gross domestic product in billions of United States dollars ($ billion).
Data source: Oxford Economics. 2016. *Global Cities 2030*. Oxford Global Headquarters.

How the Mumbai Metro Can Empower through Equal Access for All

The Mumbai Metro will have several facilities for women commuters to make their travel safe:
- provision of surveillance cameras installed inside trains;
- nursing and breastfeeding room facilities at each station;
- separate hygienic toilets for women at each station;
- installation of sanitary pad dispensing machines;
- separate ticket counters and vending machines for women;
- use of mobile apps to disseminate information related to women's safety;
- 15% allocated spaces in metro stations owned (or operated) by women, in addition to dedicated carriages for women passengers;
- dedicated seats for women in each coach;
- installation of closed circuit TV cameras at every metro station;
- day care centers at selected stations; and
- pilot station having all-women staff.

Friendly features of the Mumbai Metro for the vulnerable groups. The Mumbai Metro offers some safety and accessibility features and facilities to assist women, the elderly, and other vulnerable groups (images are illustrative taken from photos by Peretz Partensky, as posted in *Flickr*; Mario Roberto Durán Ortiz, as posted in *Wikimedia Commons*; Prinz.W, as posted in *Wikimedia Commons*; and Bill William Compton, as posted in *Wikimedia Commons*).

The Mumbai Metro will also provide several facilities to the differently abled and improve accessibility for them. It is planned to have allocated space for wheelchairs in trains, platform-level boarding, elevators, escalators, accessibility ramps, allocated waiting areas at each station, dedicated seats for the physically disabled passengers in each coach, and priority e-ticketing counters, among other facilities.

The Mumbai Metro lines can provide the vulnerable groups in Mumbai with easy accessibility to a number of socioeconomic centers of development like education institutes, health-care facilities, etc. This accessibility, as shown in Maps 10 and 11, can provide the people of the MMR to easily use these facilities and eventually improve the key socioeconomic indexes like literacy, health, and employment.

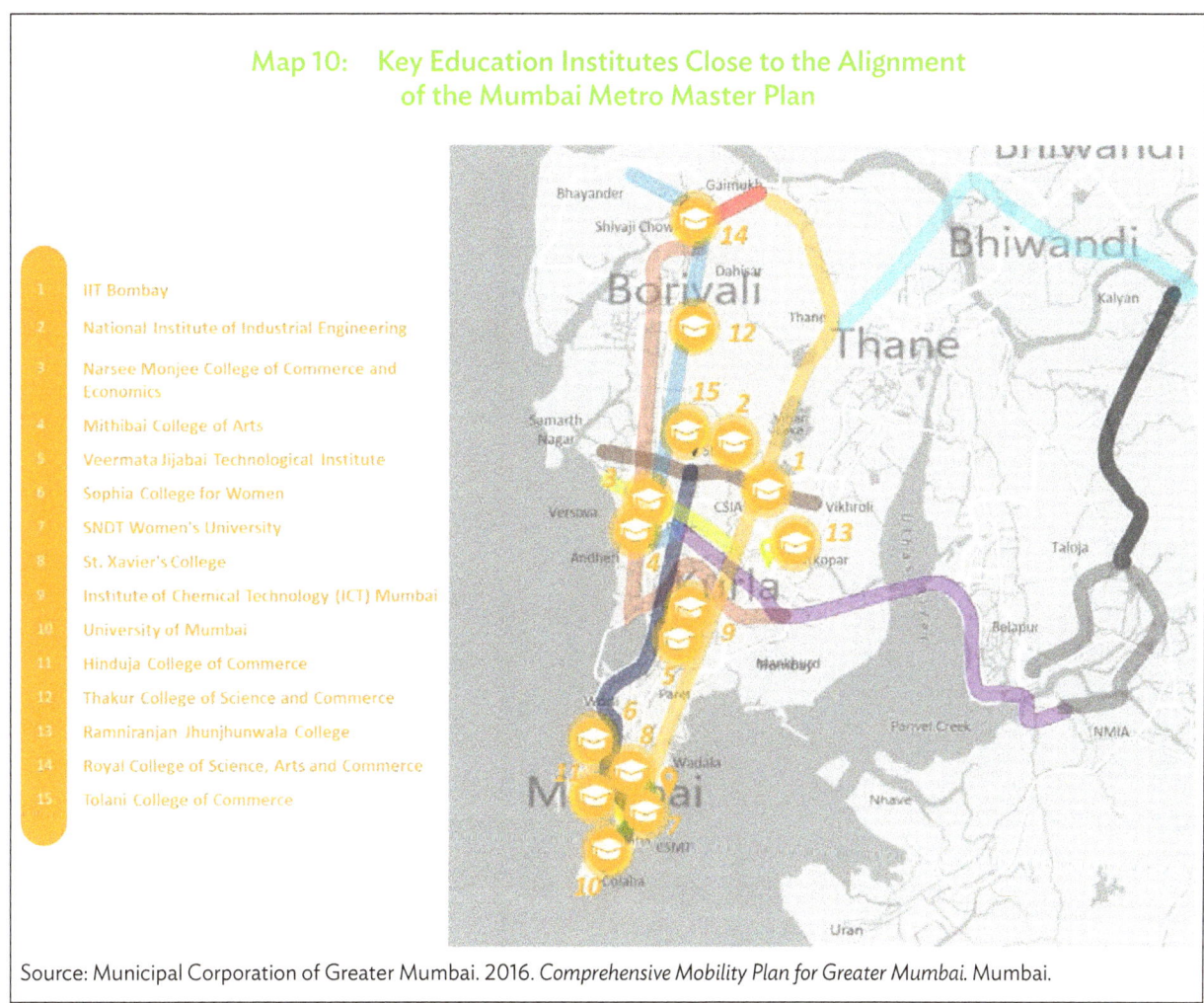

Map 10: Key Education Institutes Close to the Alignment of the Mumbai Metro Master Plan

1. IIT Bombay
2. National Institute of Industrial Engineering
3. Narsee Monjee College of Commerce and Economics
4. Mithibai College of Arts
5. Veermata Jijabai Technological Institute
6. Sophia College for Women
7. SNDT Women's University
8. St. Xavier's College
9. Institute of Chemical Technology (ICT) Mumbai
10. University of Mumbai
11. Hinduja College of Commerce
12. Thakur College of Science and Commerce
13. Ramniranjan Jhunjhunwala College
14. Royal College of Science, Arts and Commerce
15. Tolani College of Commerce

Source: Municipal Corporation of Greater Mumbai. 2016. *Comprehensive Mobility Plan for Greater Mumbai*. Mumbai.

A survey for assessing the passenger satisfaction on the Mumbai Metro Line 1, undertaken by a special-purpose vehicle called the Mumbai Metro One Private Limited (MMOPL), indicates the positive impact of the metro rail system. The survey consisted of more than 2,000 commuters from various ages, genders, socioeconomic profiles, times of day, stations, etc. Of the respondents, 85% rated the overall experience highly (with a mean score of almost 89%, exceeding the set norm of 84%). Further, 91% of the respondents gave positive ratings for cleanliness at the metro stations and trains. The same group gave very low cleanliness ratings to other modes of public transport, such as only 17% for the Brihanmumbai Electricity Supply and Transport (BEST) buses and only 9% for the Mumbai suburban trains. In fact, 95% of the respondents were willing to recommend the metro train service to other commuters.[12] Not surprisingly, the passenger groups that had the greatest satisfaction levels were women, as well as commuters aged 60 years and above (Figure 17). Thus, the Mumbai Metro has already started providing better accessibility options to the vulnerable groups, and this benefit is expected to increase multifold as more metro lines get operationalized.

---

[12] Kadence International. 2015. *Mumbai Metro Line 1 Survey*. Mumbai.

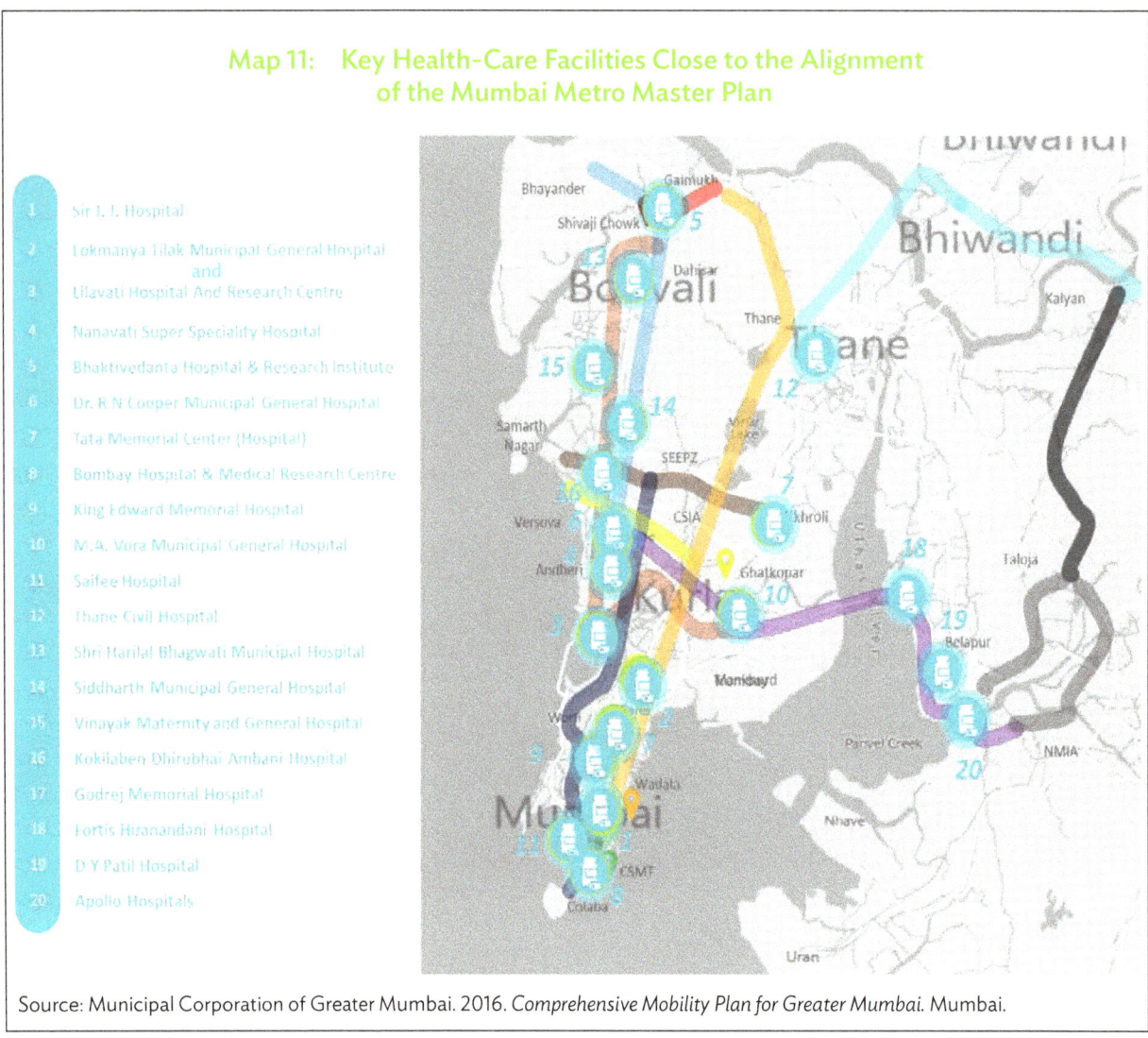

Source: Municipal Corporation of Greater Mumbai. 2016. *Comprehensive Mobility Plan for Greater Mumbai*. Mumbai.

To further provide a modern and high-quality commuter experience to everyone, Mumbai Metro Line 1 has already released the Mumbai Metro I app. The app can help in recharging travel cards and can also function as a travel planner.

The economic benefits of Mumbai Metro Lines 2A, 2B, and 7, quantified in terms of savings in time (due to better accessibility), are expected to be twofold: (i) the time savings for people who will shift from road to the metro rail system; and (ii) the time savings for people who will continue to use the road network, but with less congestion.

The first benefit is expected to come from reduced travel time of the metro journeys as compared to the road-based journeys. The second benefit is expected to come from the reduced travel time for road traffic. The introduction of the metro rail transit system in Mumbai is expected to reduce road congestion, which in turn will increase the average speed on the road network. Thus, people travelling on the roads in Mumbai (after the introduction of the metro) will be able to reach their respective destinations faster, as quantified in Figure 18.

Figure 17: Results of Commuter Satisfaction Survey for Mumbai Metro Line 1, 2014

85% high overall experience

91% positive ratings for cleanliness

95% will recommend metro to other commuters

 groups with the highest satisfaction scores

Data source: TNN. 2014. 85% Passengers Satisfied with Metro. *The Times of India*. 29 July.

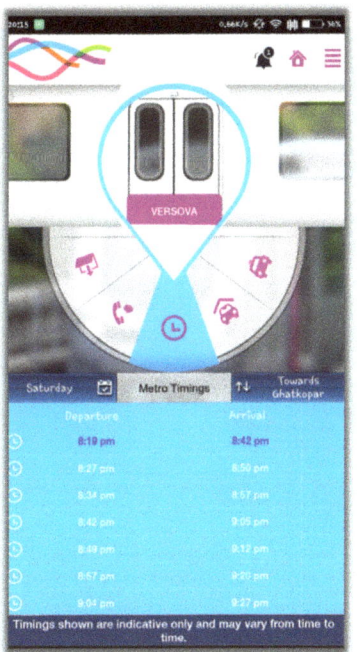
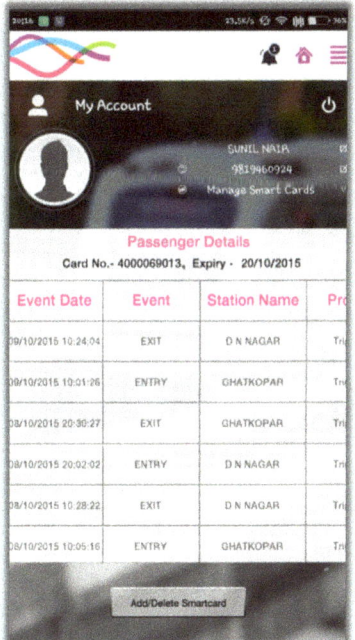
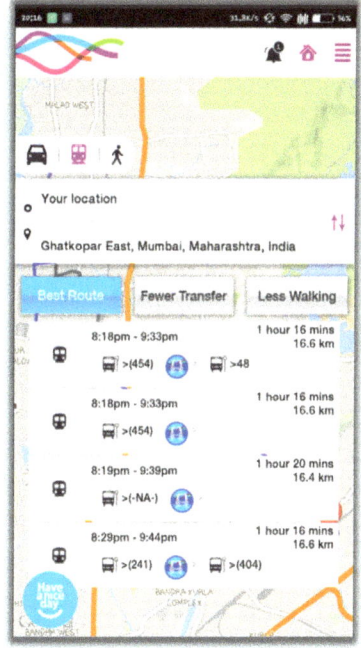

Mumbai Metro I app. The mobile application features a travel planner and provides information on the bus and local train networks in Mumbai, fares, travel history, smart card balance, and latest offerings and promotions (photos by Mumbai Metro One Private Limited).

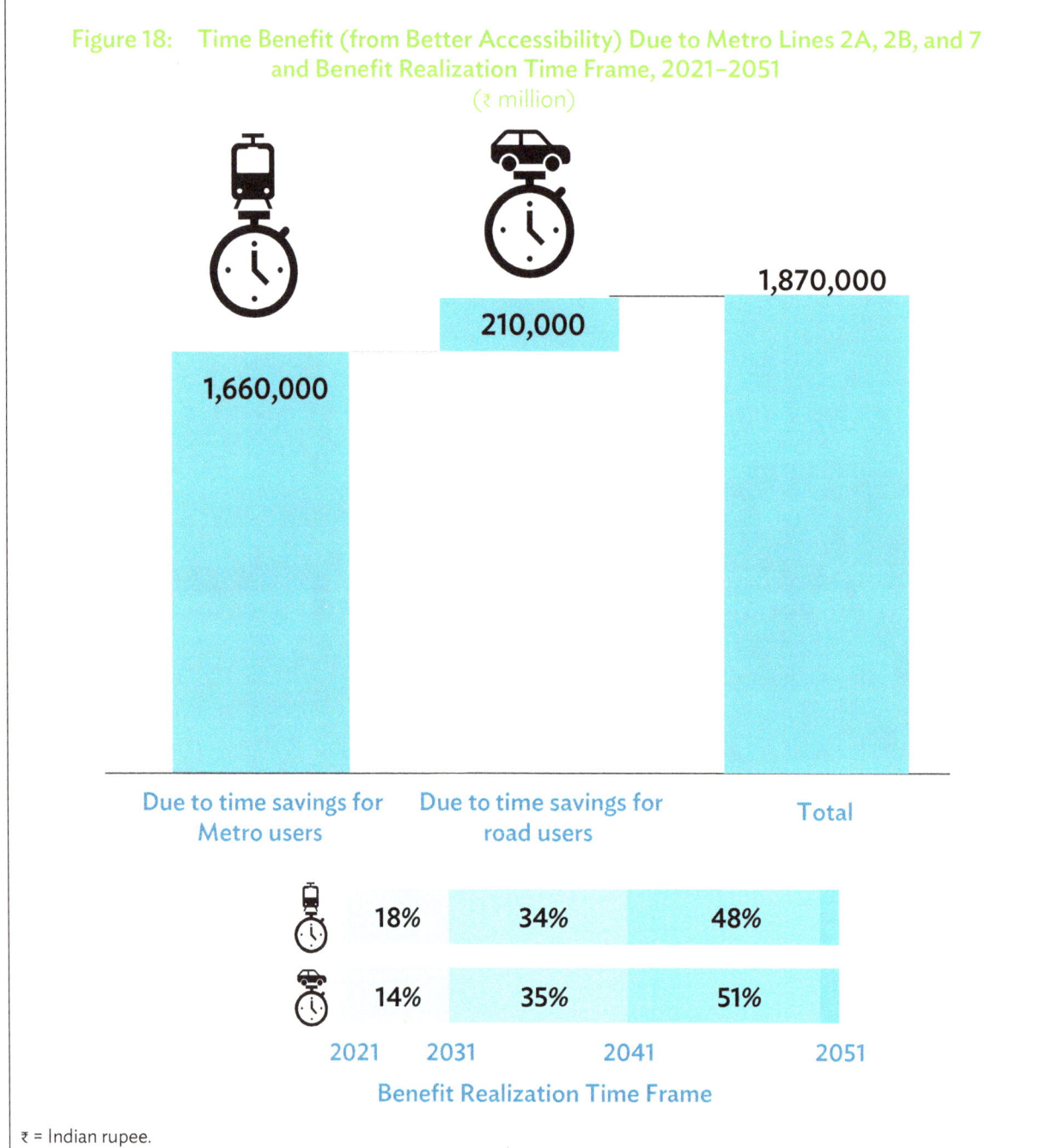

Figure 18: Time Benefit (from Better Accessibility) Due to Metro Lines 2A, 2B, and 7 and Benefit Realization Time Frame, 2021–2051
(₹ million)

₹ = Indian rupee.
Data source: Asian Development Bank. 2019. *Report and Recommendation of the President to the Board of Directors: Proposed Loan to India for the Mumbai Metro Rail Systems Project*. Economic Analysis (accessible from the list of linked documents in Appendix 2). Manila.

The accessibility benefits of the Mumbai Metro (derived from the savings in travel time) are expected to be sustained into the future (benefits up to 2051 have been shown in Figure 18). Importantly, they are expected to increase strongly with each passing decade, and the time and accessibility benefits in 2041–2051 are expected to be more than 2.5 times those in 2021–2031.

The benefits shown in Figure 18 are for only two Metro lines (i.e., Lines 2 and 7) in the overall master plan. The realization of the entire Mumbai Metro Master Plan, therefore, is expected to generate multifold benefits for the city of Mumbai.

Suburban train in Mumbai. Overcrowding leads to unsafe conditions, such as passengers hanging outside the trains (photo by Stefan in *Flickr*).

Contributing toward a Safer City

Passenger Safety—Life on the Lifeline

The most important aspect of any transportation network is the safety of its passengers. Networks that offer safer modes of transportation are strongly favored by passengers. Since commuters in the Mumbai Metropolitan Region (MMR) use both road-based and suburban rail-based modes of transport, it is important to understand the level of safety offered by both of these modes. Safety is measured and compared in terms of fatalities per annum, which establishes a baseline.

More than 50% of the modal share of commuter trips in Mumbai is derived from road-based modes of transportation, such as the Brihanmumbai Electricity Supply and Transport (BEST) buses, taxis, auto-rickshaws, private cars, and two-wheelers. Thus, it is important to understand the safety offered on the road networks in India as well as Mumbai on both global and national levels. An analysis of the World Health Organization (WHO) dataset (covering more than 175 countries) on the number of road-traffic deaths per annum indicates that India has more than 150,000 deaths. As seen in Figure 19, this is the highest number in the world and is worse by 2.5 times than that of the second-ranked country.[13]

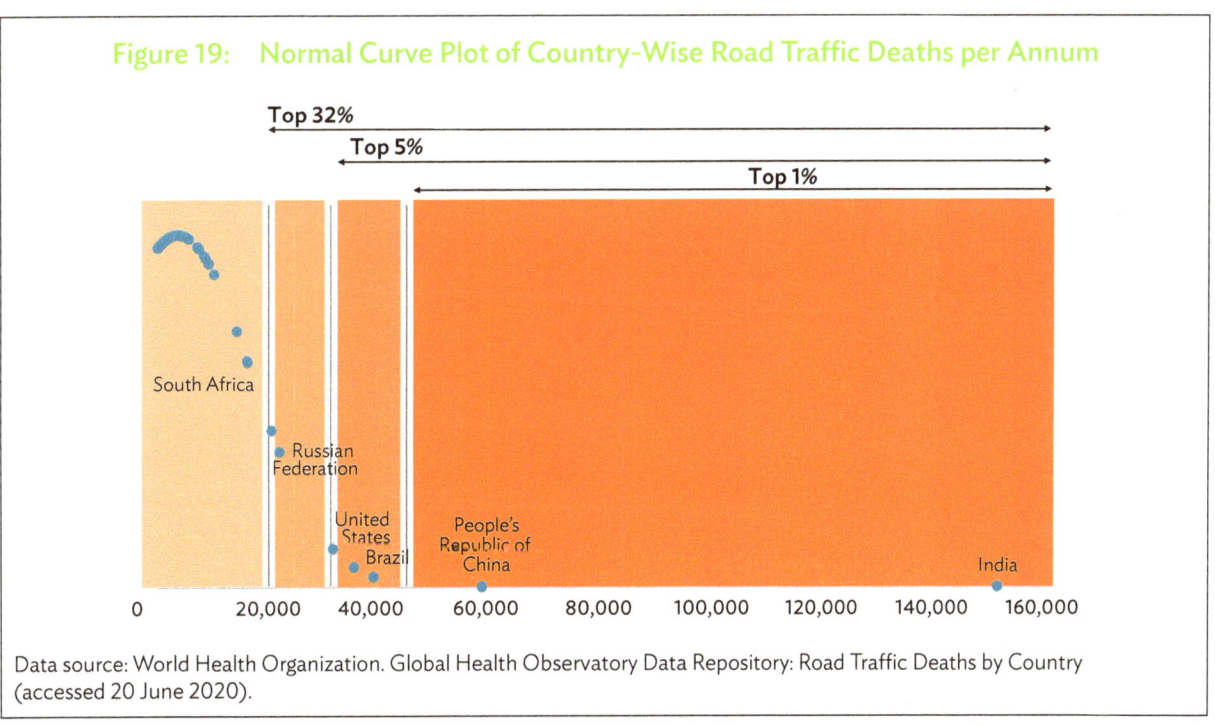

Figure 19: Normal Curve Plot of Country-Wise Road Traffic Deaths per Annum

Data source: World Health Organization. Global Health Observatory Data Repository: Road Traffic Deaths by Country (accessed 20 June 2020).

---

[13] World Health Organization. Global Health Observatory Data Repository: Road Traffic Deaths by Country (accessed 20 June 2020).

Further, the same dataset indicates that the number of Indian road-traffic deaths is also high, at 226 per million population. This metric for India is not only worse when compared to developed countries like the United States, the United Kingdom, Germany, France, and Japan, where the metrics range from 31 to 124 road-traffic deaths per million population, but it is also worse than the metrics for BRICS nations, which range from 180 to 196 road-traffic deaths per million population.

A deeper, city-level analysis of road networks in India provides key insights on their relative safety. As can be seen in Figure 20, Mumbai is in the top 10 most unsafe cities in India for road-based transportation, despite its relatively higher patronage of public transportation.[14] The risk exposure on the roads in Mumbai, measured in terms of number of accidents and fatalities from these accidents per annum, is relatively high; hence, passengers on the road network are constantly seeking safer options for transportation.

An analysis of the safety on the suburban railway network also merits consideration since it has the highest individual modal share (more than 40%) of all commuter journeys in Mumbai. Suburban railway is the lifeline of the people of Mumbai, but it has a high number of railway fatalities per annum (Figure 21). During the 5-year period ending in 2015, more than 11 deaths per day were reported on the Mumbai suburban network.[15]

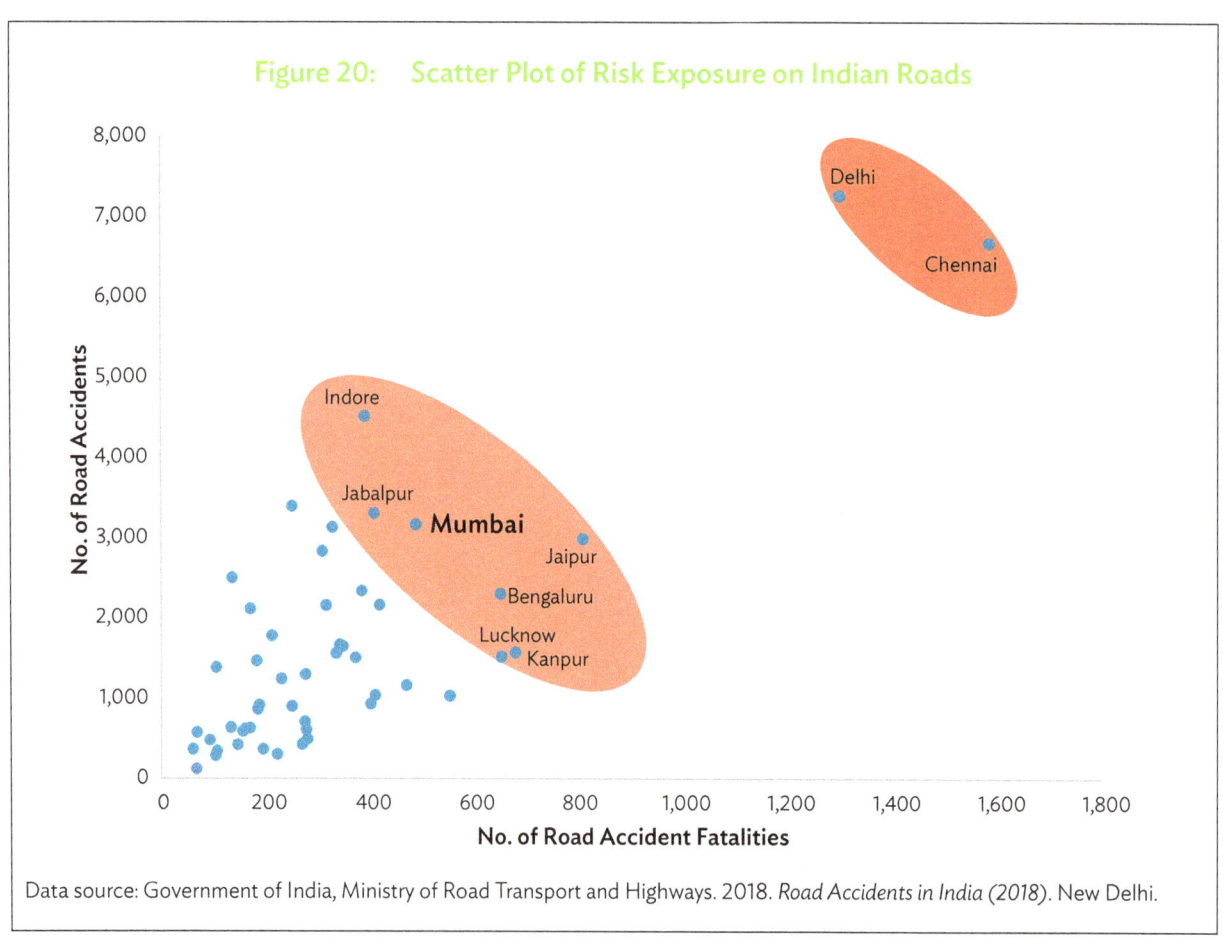

Figure 20: Scatter Plot of Risk Exposure on Indian Roads

Data source: Government of India, Ministry of Road Transport and Highways. 2018. *Road Accidents in India (2018)*. New Delhi.

---

[14] Government of India, Ministry of Road Transport and Highways. 2018. *Road Accidents in India (2018)*. New Delhi.
[15] Government of India, Comptroller and Auditor General. 2016. *Report 14 of 2016 - Union Railways Performance Audit Suburban Train Services in Indian Railways*. New Delhi.

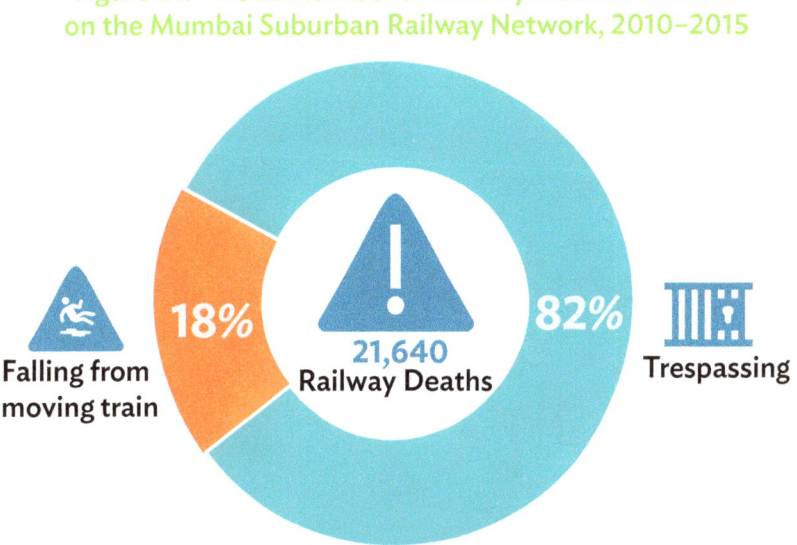

Data source: Government of India, Comptroller and Auditor General. 2016. *Report 14 of 2016 - Union Railways Performance Audit Suburban Train Services in Indian Railways*. New Delhi.

Out of a total of 33,445 deaths on the suburban Indian Railways network (Central Zone, Eastern Zone, South Eastern Zone, South Central Zone, Southern Zone, Western Zone, Mumbai, and Kolkata), 17,638 occurred on the Mumbai suburban network due to trespassing and 4,002 due to falling from moving trains. These data for the 5-year period indicate that trespassing is the single biggest cause (82%) of rail-related accidents on the Mumbai suburban network, followed by people falling from moving trains (18%).

The hazards of train commuting in Mumbai. Passengers are susceptible to falling for hanging outside a moving and overcrowded train (photo by Rishabh Mathur in *Flickr*).

Suburban railway station in Mumbai. Overcrowding in the suburban railway stations and trains is among the major transport-related issues in Mumbai (photo by Rajarshi Mitra in *Flickr*).

As detailed previously, the suburban rail network is under tremendous demand pressure. There is extreme crowding within the trains and on the railway stations. A horrendous stampede happened at the Elphinstone railway station that killed 23 people and injured several others in 2017.

It should be noted that road and rail authorities in Mumbai are constantly undertaking improvements to enhance the safety of their respective transport networks. Measures and proposals like the introduction of the communication-based train control system on the suburban network, removal of 24 seats from some coaches so that additional 224 standing commuters can be accommodated (instead of commuters hanging by the train), construction and strengthening of footbridges, and safety audits of 445 road overpasses and footbridges have improved the safety of the networks—but more steps are needed. These measures have resulted in decreasing the number of railway fatalities to almost seven per day (2018–2019).[16] However, this number still needs to be decreased significantly and eventually brought down to zero on a sustainable basis.

Mumbai Monsoons—A Transport Challenge

Mumbai faces heavy rains of more than 2,000 millimeters per annum, out of which more than 1,600 millimeters occur during the annual monsoons from June to August.[17] Monsoon rains inundate the roads and the railway tracks in Mumbai because of a choking drainage system, rising sea levels, and extensive land reclamation.

This inundation and waterlogging bring transport in the city to a grinding halt every year. Mumbai suburban rail passengers face issues like train delays, train derailments, and even cancellations of services, leaving thousands of commuters stranded frequently during these months. Similarly, travelers using the BEST buses also face breakdowns and severe traffic jams.

---

[16] S. Sen. 2019. Mumbai: Suburban Railway Deaths Drop by 10%. *The Times of India.* 4 January.
[17] Government of India, Ministry of Earth Sciences, India Meteorological Department. 2017. *Rainfall Statistics of India - 2016.* New Delhi.

Operating conditions of flooded roads in Mumbai. Surface-based modes of transport come to a halt during the heavy Mumbai monsoons because of excessive rainfall and waterlogging (photo by Inexplicable in *Flickr*).

Other modes of transport such as autos, taxis, and private vehicles also get stuck in long jams on the congested roads, while the surge pricing levied by cab aggregators makes on-demand cabs unviable for many commuters. Thus, heavy monsoon rains severely impact the transportation options for the people in Mumbai. Passengers have to surmount the risk and fear of accidents on the road and suburban railway networks in Mumbai during the monsoons in order to get normal day-to-day things done. Thus, there is a need for a safe and reliable mode of public transport that can help transport the people of Mumbai even during the monsoon period.

How the Mumbai Metro Can Provide a Safe Transport Option

The biggest reason for fatalities on the existing modes of public transport in Mumbai is trespassing on the railway tracks. Trespassing occurs when people do not wait for the incoming train to pass and risk crossing the tracks from unauthorized points. Since the existing suburban network is almost entirely at grade, the incidences of railway track trespassing are high. The second most important reason for fatalities is people falling from moving trains or getting struck by objects like poles, while hanging onto the trains. These incidents occur because the extremely overcrowded coaches of the Mumbai suburban trains do not have doors. The coaches are open by design and leave an option for desperate commuters on the already overcrowded trains to hang by and reach their destination, albeit risking their lives. The extreme overcrowding at the suburban stations also leads to a lot of unavoidable commotion at the platform queues. This sometimes results in accidents like pushing and falling on the track of the incoming train.

The Mumbai Metro trains will eliminate the root causes of the above fatalities by their very design (Figure 22). Since the metro trains will be either elevated or underground, there will be no possibility for anyone crossing over the tracks. Further, the metro train sets have doors that close as soon as the train starts moving. This should prevent the occurrence of people hanging outside the trains. Another key design element of metro trains, i.e., the platform screen doors, should protect people from accidentally being pushed onto the tracks while waiting for the trains. This physical barrier between the passenger waiting on the platform and the tracks for the incoming train only opens when the train has arrived.

The elevated tracks of the metro rail transit system will also ensure avoidance of waterlogging that happens at the ground level. This is expected to provide safe, reliable, and continuous operations even during heavy rains in Mumbai. The Mumbai Metro trains will also have GoA4 automation, where trains will be capable of automatic operations, including door closing and obstacle detection.

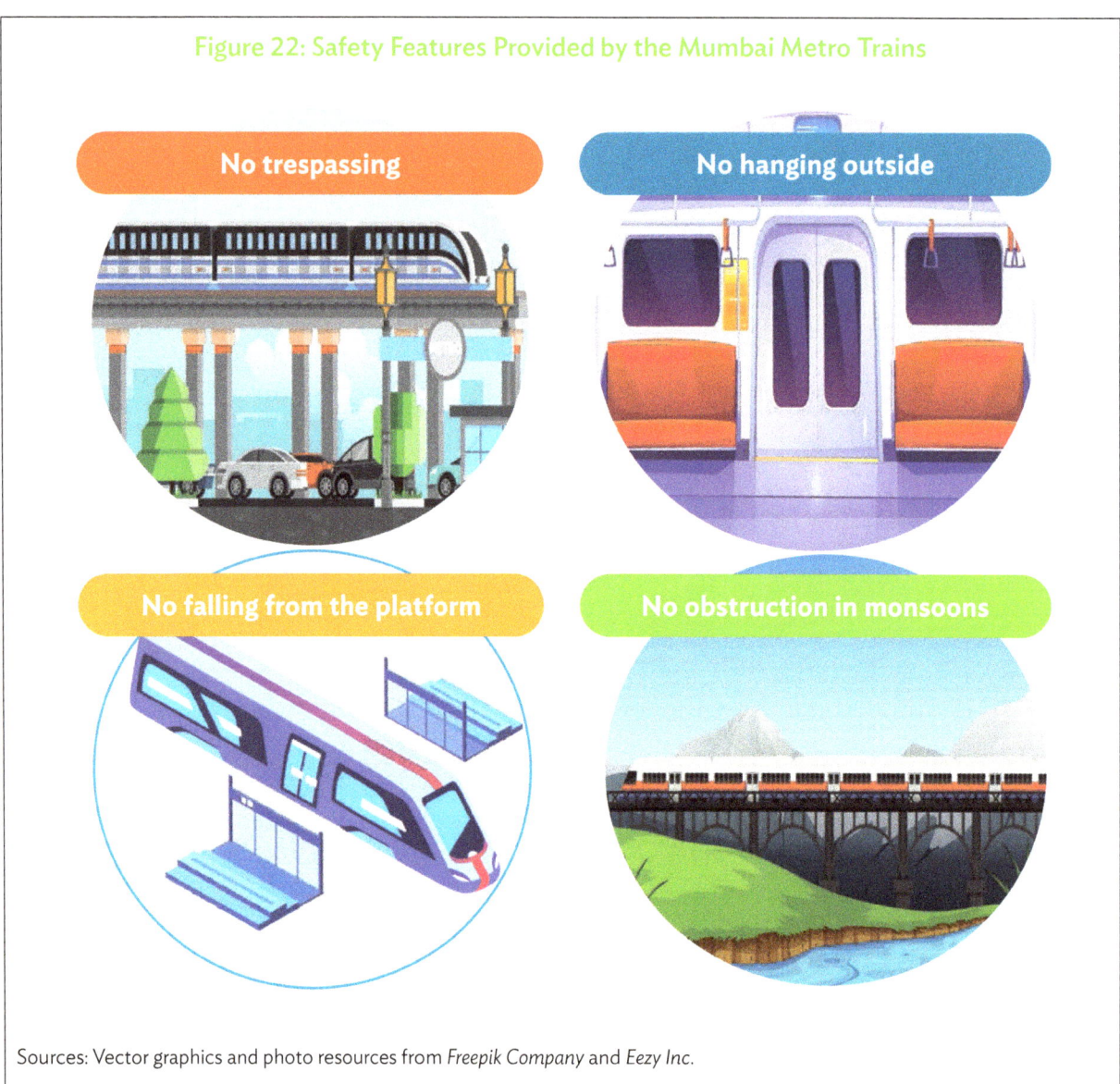

Figure 22: Safety Features Provided by the Mumbai Metro Trains

Sources: Vector graphics and photo resources from *Freepik Company* and *Eezy Inc*.

The safety benefits of Lines 2A, 2B, and 7 have been quantified in terms of reduced rail and road accidents (due to the modal shift to metro). The benefits shown in Figure 23 are for only two Metro lines (i.e., Lines 2 and 7) in the Mumbai Metro Master Plan, the full realization of which will generate numerous benefits for Mumbai City.

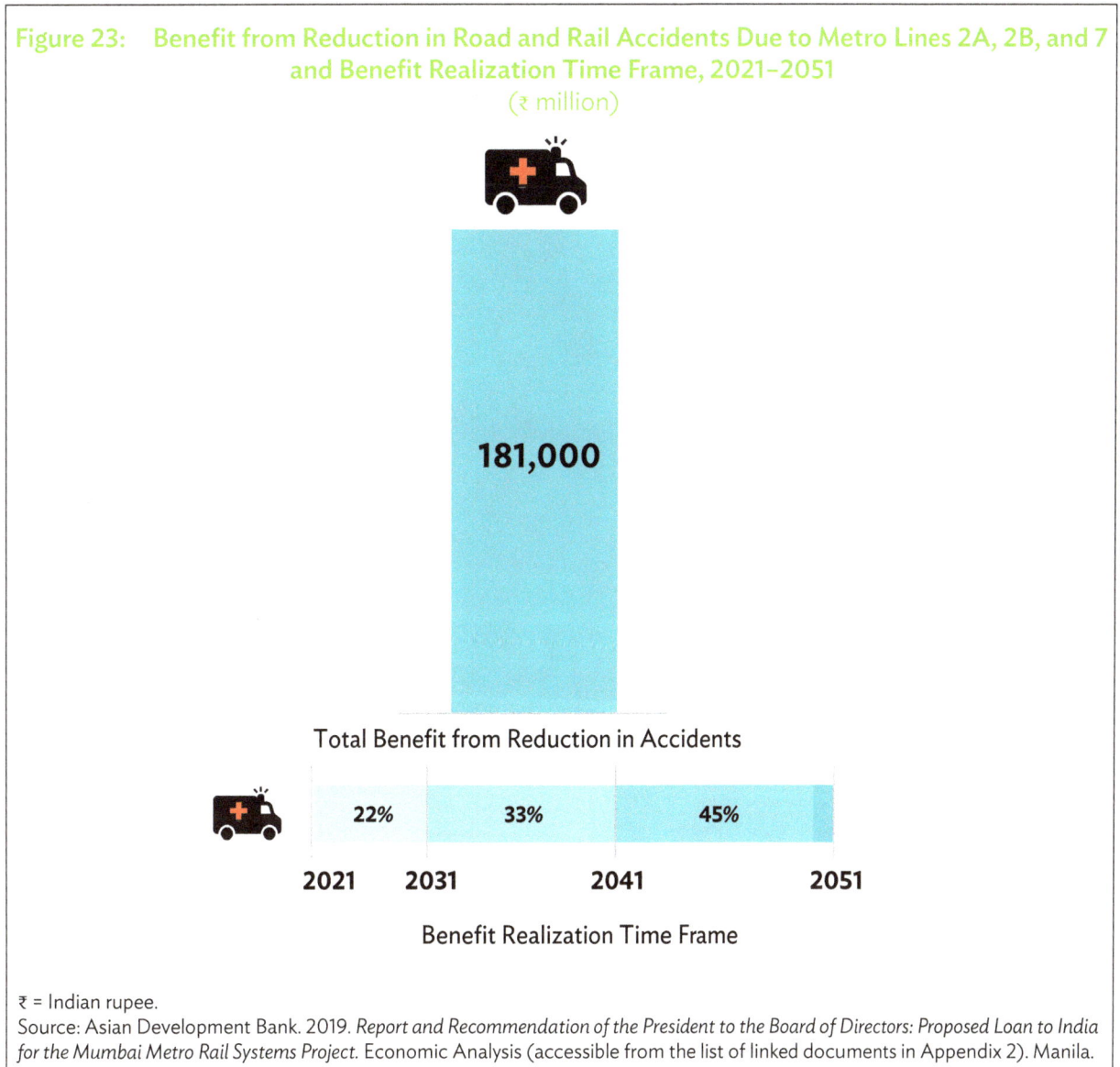

Figure 23: Benefit from Reduction in Road and Rail Accidents Due to Metro Lines 2A, 2B, and 7 and Benefit Realization Time Frame, 2021–2051
(₹ million)

₹ = Indian rupee.
Source: Asian Development Bank. 2019. *Report and Recommendation of the President to the Board of Directors: Proposed Loan to India for the Mumbai Metro Rail Systems Project.* Economic Analysis (accessible from the list of linked documents in Appendix 2). Manila.

Pollution in Mumbai. The city wears a hazy look due to pollution at specific times of the year (photo by Honza Soukup in *Flickr*).

Contributing toward a Cleaner City

Air Pollution in Mumbai—A Global Perspective

According to WHO, air pollution is a major cause of death, from stroke to lung cancer and heart diseases. It has severe negative effects on human health, especially that of children and senior citizens. One of the biggest reasons for this adverse health impact is the presence of a mix of organic and chemical particulate matter (PM) suspended in the air. PM particles are extremely small (often measured in microns) and, hence, are easily breathable. This makes PM extremely dangerous as it can penetrate deep into the respiratory tract and cause severe health damages. $PM_{2.5}$ is the breathable particulate matter that is 2.5 microns in diameter or smaller. Individuals, families, and businesses are increasingly preferring to locate to cities where the PM is within acceptable limits.

An analysis of WHO's air quality database, which measures the mean annual exposure to $PM_{2.5}$ particles in micrograms per cubic meter ($\mu g/m^3$), indicates the position of Mumbai with respect to 3,000 cities in the world. This data, plotted on a normal curve, shows that Mumbai is in the top 5% most polluted cities in the world (Figure 24). Based on the data, the annual $PM_{2.5}$ measure in Mumbai (64 $\mu g/m^3$) is 3–5 times when compared

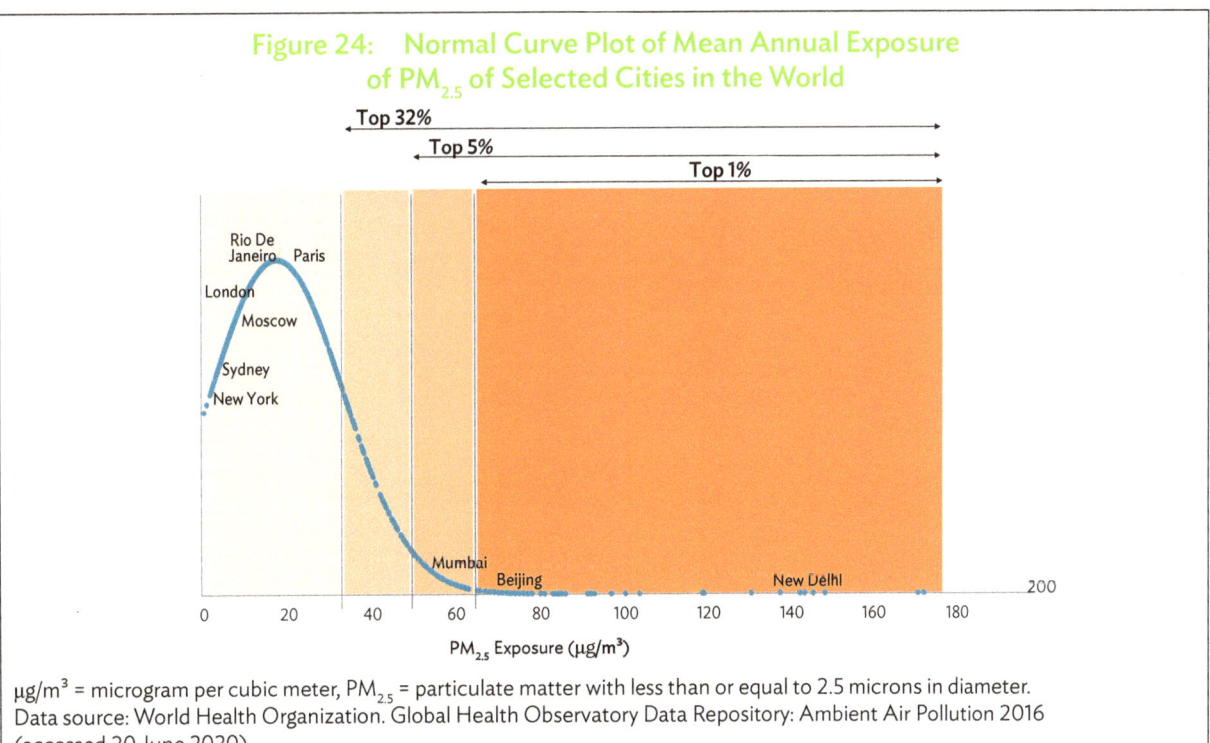

Figure 24: Normal Curve Plot of Mean Annual Exposure of $PM_{2.5}$ of Selected Cities in the World

$\mu g/m^3$ = microgram per cubic meter, $PM_{2.5}$ = particulate matter with less than or equal to 2.5 microns in diameter.
Data source: World Health Organization. Global Health Observatory Data Repository: Ambient Air Pollution 2016 (accessed 20 June 2020).

with global cities around the world—e.g., New York (7 µg/m³), London (12 µg/m³), and Paris (16 µg/m³). Further, the $PM_{2.5}$ measure in Mumbai is more than 3 times the world average of 18 µg/m³ and more than 6 times the safe limit prescribed by WHO at 10 µg/m³.[18]

Major $PM_{2.5}$ Red Zones within Mumbai

A deeper understanding of the $PM_{2.5}$ emissions scenario in Mumbai can improve sustainability. The $PM_{2.5}$ measure in key areas within Mumbai highlights the specific red zones, as graphically represented in Map 12. For 2019, the highest $PM_{2.5}$ measure in Mumbai was observed in Bandra Kurla Complex (86 µg/m³), followed by Andheri (79 µg/m³). Both areas have a $PM_{2.5}$ measure that is 25% higher than the average of Mumbai.[19]

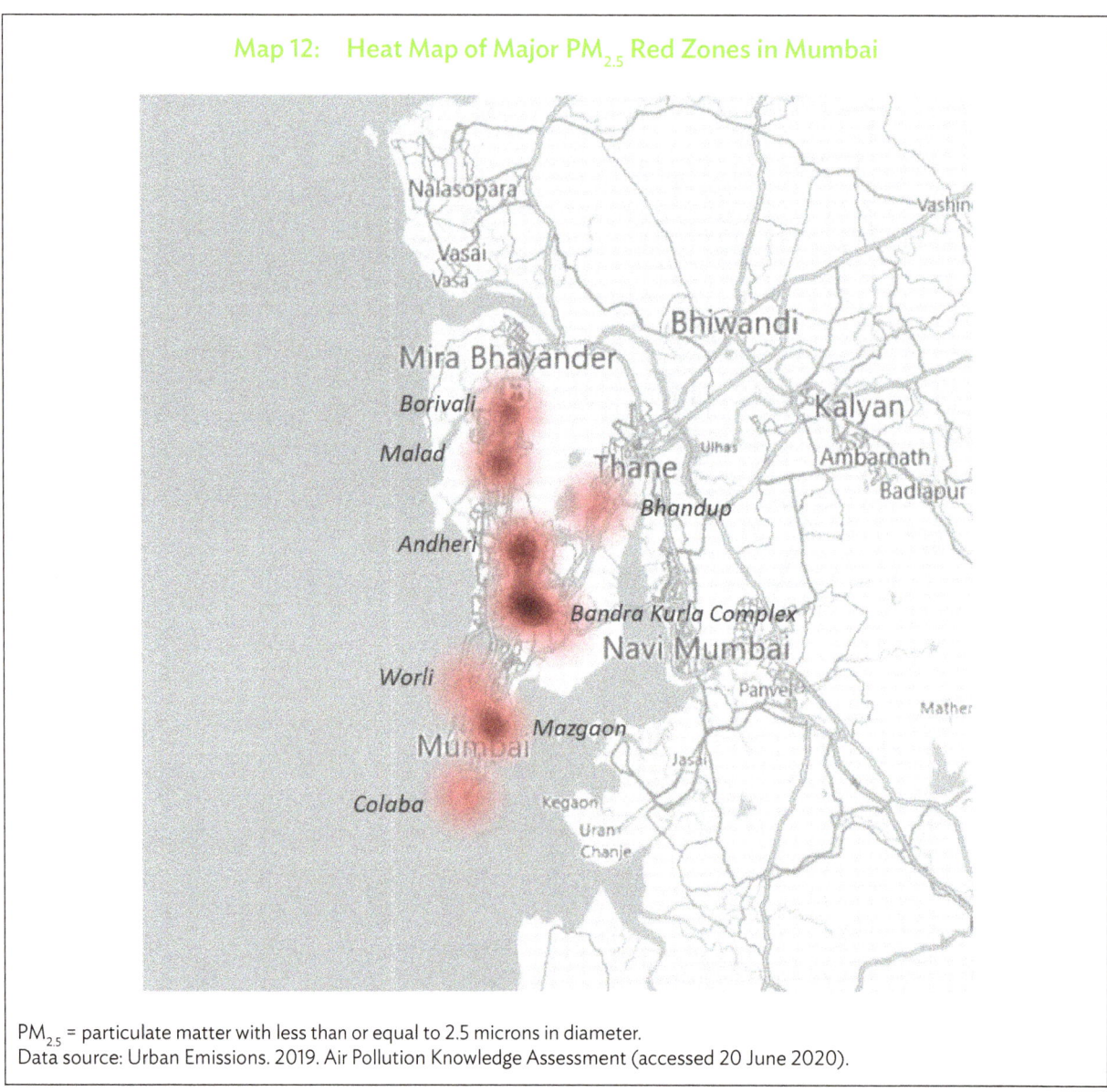

Map 12: Heat Map of Major $PM_{2.5}$ Red Zones in Mumbai

$PM_{2.5}$ = particulate matter with less than or equal to 2.5 microns in diameter.
Data source: Urban Emissions. 2019. Air Pollution Knowledge Assessment (accessed 20 June 2020).

---

[18] World Health Organization. Global Health Observatory Data Repository: Ambient Air Pollution 2016 (accessed 20 June 2020).
[19] Urban Emissions. 2019. Air Pollution Knowledge Assessment (accessed 20 June 2020).

In order for Mumbai to position itself as a sustainable city of the future, it must reduce its pollution level, with specific focus on the above red zones. Lower air pollution can enable Mumbai to further attract world-class talent and compete with other major cities of the world.

Biggest Contributor to $PM_{2.5}$ Emissions in Mumbai

In 2018, the two biggest contributors toward the overall $PM_{2.5}$ emissions in Mumbai are industrial emissions (42%) and transport (26%), as shown in Figure 25. It is projected that, given the status quo in 2030, transport emissions will become the biggest contributor to $PM_{2.5}$ emissions in Mumbai, with a 35% contribution, followed by industrial emissions. Further, other pollutant emissions like carbon monoxide and volatile organic compounds from transportation are also observed to be 10 and 3 times higher, respectively, than industrial emissions. Thus, the most significant contributor for controlling $PM_{2.5}$ emissions in Mumbai, and reducing the air pollution, will be controlling the transport-related emissions.

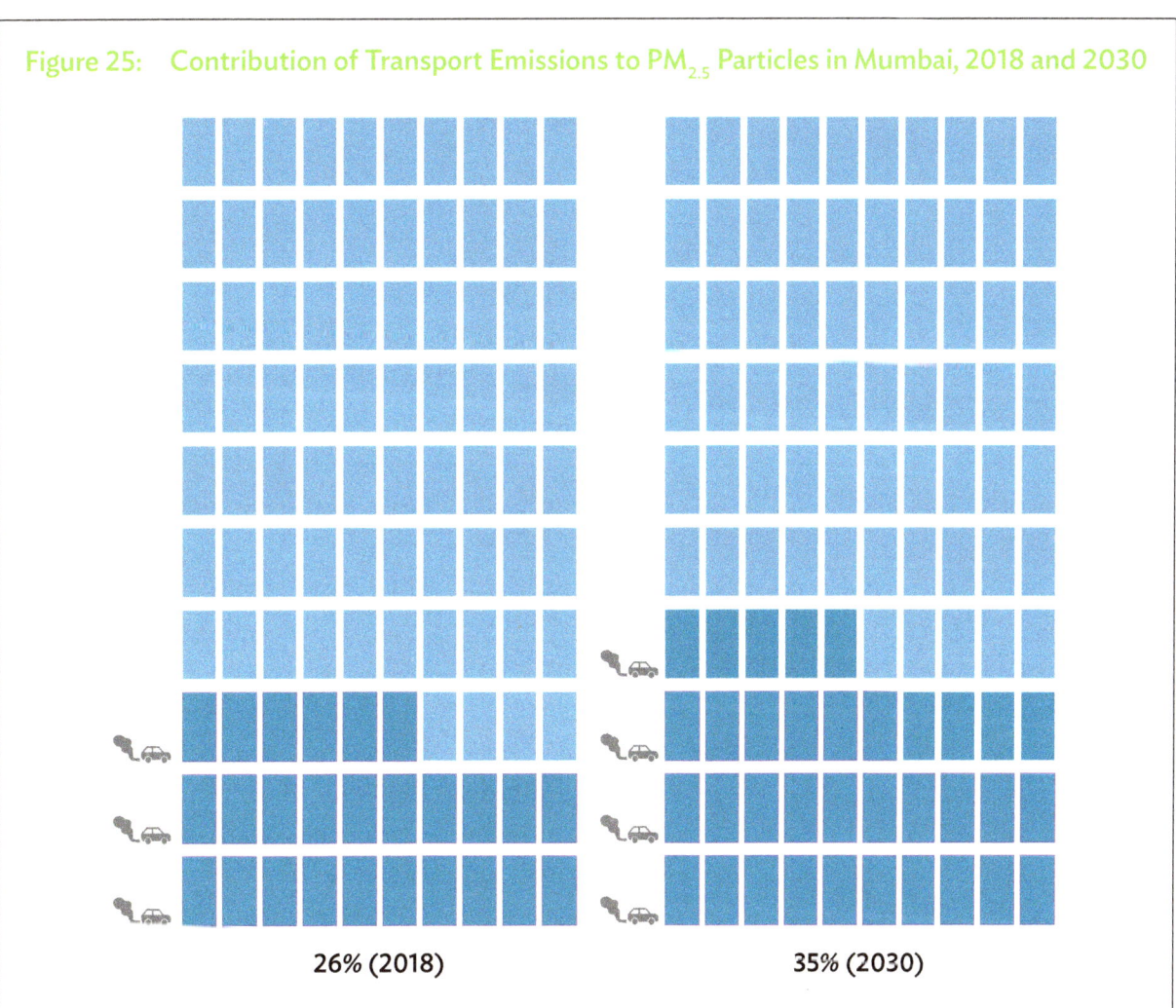

Figure 25: Contribution of Transport Emissions to $PM_{2.5}$ Particles in Mumbai, 2018 and 2030

26% (2018) 35% (2030)

$PM_{2.5}$ = particulate matter with less than or equal to 2.5 microns in diameter.
Data source: Urban Emissions. 2019. Air Pollution Knowledge Assessment (accessed 20 June 2020).

Since emissions per passenger from private modes of transport (like cars) are substantially higher than emissions from public modes of transport, it is important to understand the historical and projected growth of personal vehicles. An increase in the number of personal vehicles on the roads of Mumbai will substantially increase the city's $PM_{2.5}$ levels.

An analysis of the number of private vehicles in Mumbai relative to its population indicates a strong upward curve. In just 16 years (from 2001 to 2017), the number of private vehicles per 1,000 population has increased more than 3 times (Figure 26).

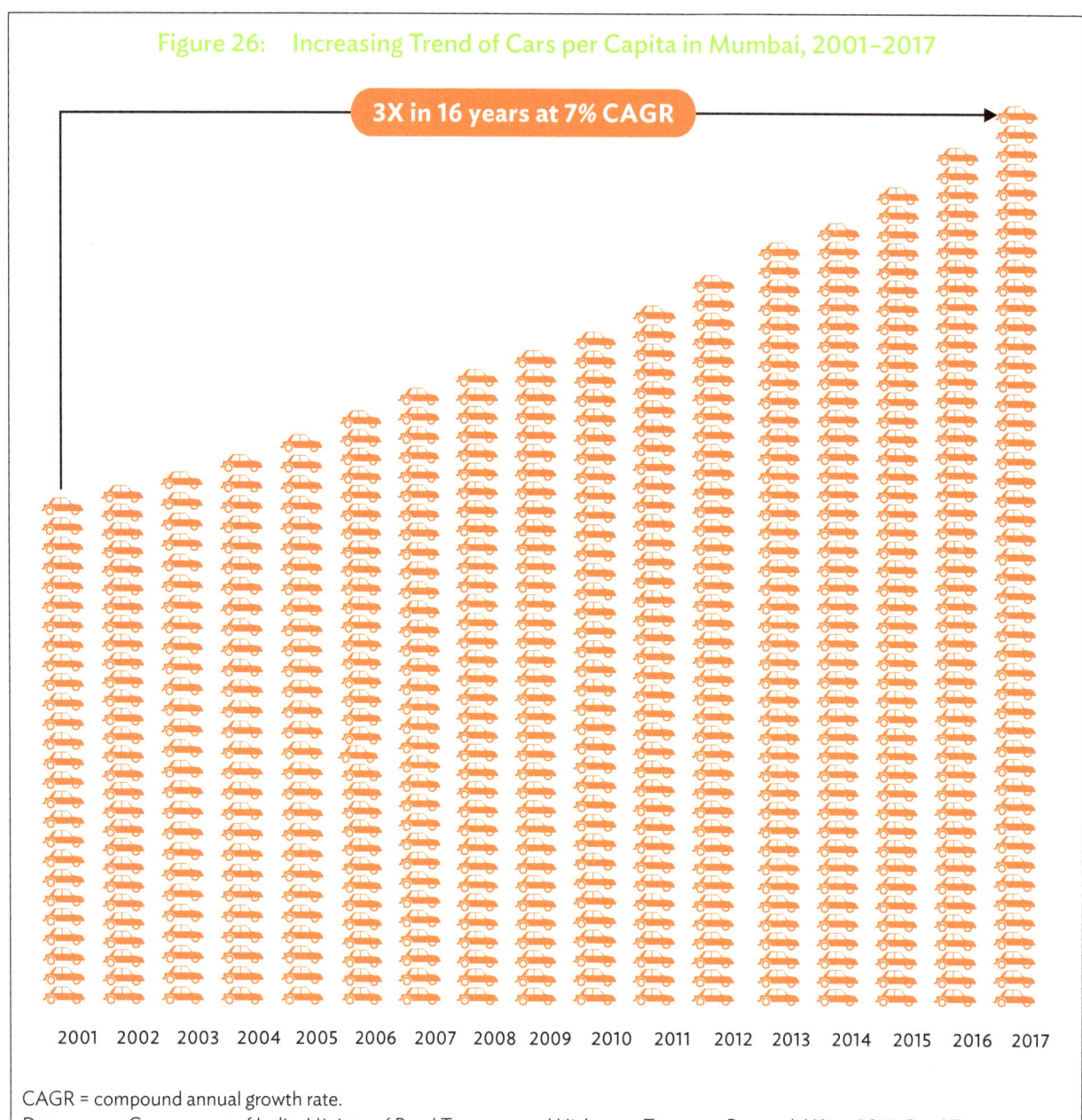

Figure 26: Increasing Trend of Cars per Capita in Mumbai, 2001–2017

3X in 16 years at 7% CAGR

CAGR = compound annual growth rate.
Data source: Government of India, Ministry of Road Transport and Highways, Transport Research Wing. 2019. *Road Transport Yearbook (2016–2017)*. New Delhi.

This increase is expected to continue in the future because cars per capita are anticipated to increase, coupled with the sustained growth in the total population of the city. According to the United Nations' World's Cities report (2018), and as depicted in Figure 27, Mumbai will be the second most populous city in India by 2030 and will be home to 28 million people, which is the current population of Australia.[20]

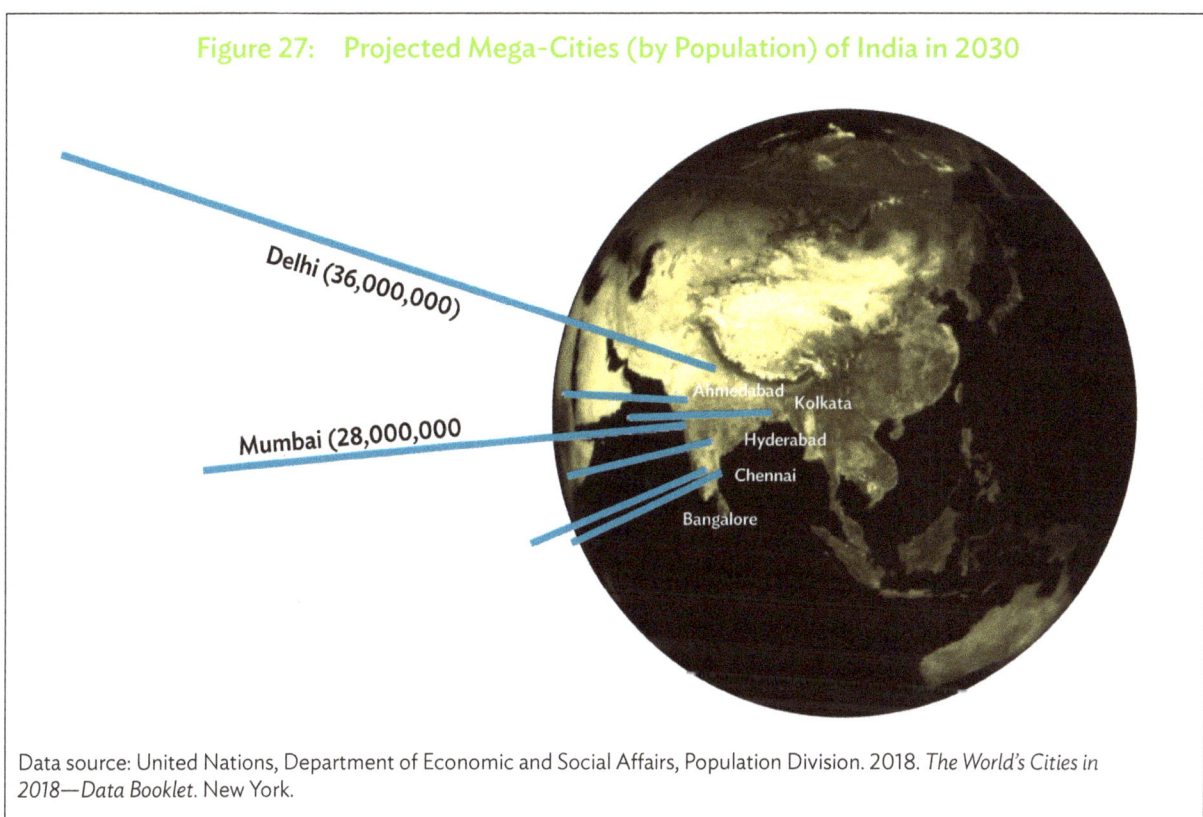

Figure 27: Projected Mega-Cities (by Population) of India in 2030

Data source: United Nations, Department of Economic and Social Affairs, Population Division. 2018. *The World's Cities in 2018—Data Booklet*. New York.

How the Mumbai Metro Can Reduce Air Pollution in Mumbai

The introduction of a metro rail transit system in Mumbai is expected to significantly change the way the people of Mumbai travel on a daily basis. As shown in Figure 28, majority of the people of Mumbai travel using the suburban rail system (43%), followed by motorized vehicles such as cars, two-wheelers, and auto-rickshaws (35%). The Brihanmumbai Electricity Supply and Transport (BEST) buses carry close to 20% of the Mumbaikars, while the existing mass transit systems like monorail and metro carry only 2% (footnote 4).

A significant reduction in $PM_{2.5}$ emissions is possible by encouraging modal shift away from motorized vehicles. As seen in Figure 28, the modal share of monorail and metro transport is projected to increase to 36% in 2031 and 42% in 2041. Specifically, Lines 2A, 2B, and 7 alone are estimated to carry close to 2 million passengers a day. This increase in modal share is expected to primarily come from the decrease in the share of motorized vehicles. The increase in modal share of the metro rail system is also expected to come from a substantial decrease in

[20] United Nations, Department of Economic and Social Affairs, Population Division. 2018. *The World's Cities in 2018—Data Booklet*. New York.

modal shares of the suburban rail and the BEST bus transportation systems. Thus, the Mumbai Metro is foreseen to control the growth of motorized vehicle trips and the consequent $PM_{2.5}$ emissions that are polluting the air in Mumbai.

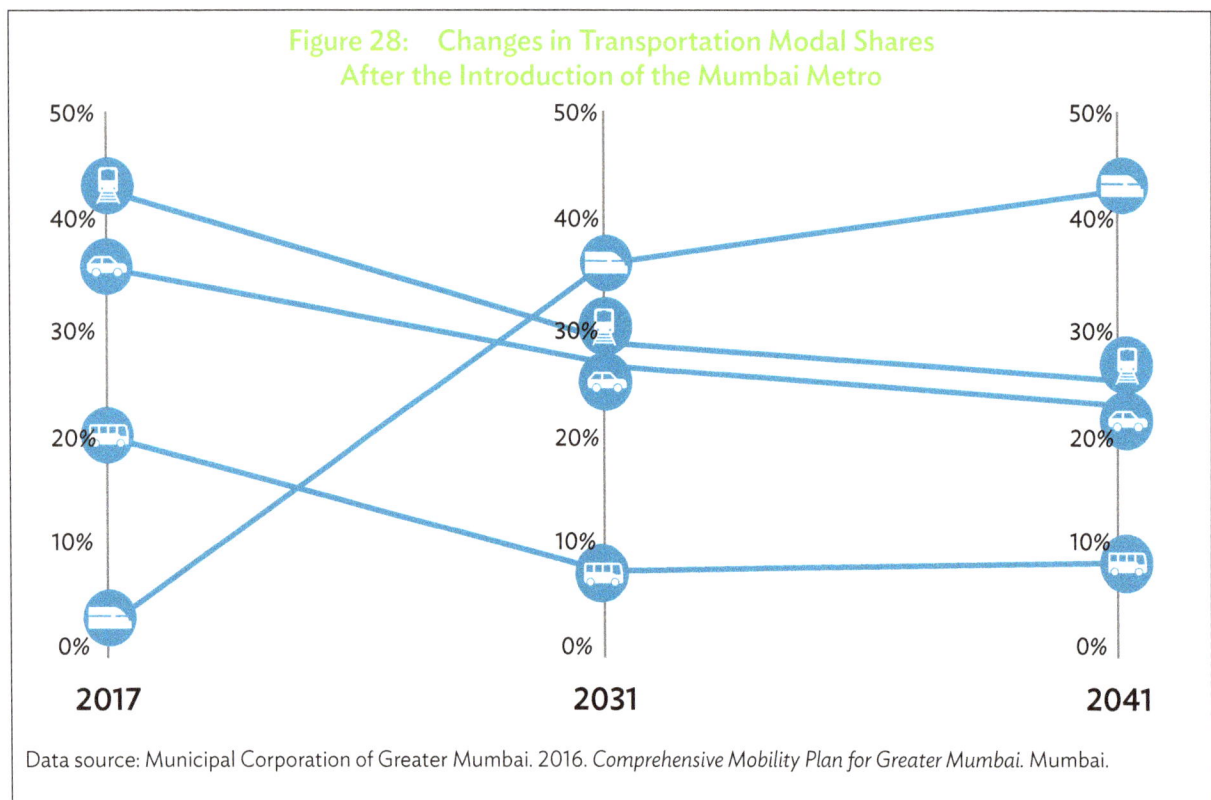

Figure 28: Changes in Transportation Modal Shares After the Introduction of the Mumbai Metro

Data source: Municipal Corporation of Greater Mumbai. 2016. *Comprehensive Mobility Plan for Greater Mumbai*. Mumbai.

Lines 2A, 2B, and 7 are reckoned to have twofold environmental benefits for the city of Mumbai. These benefits will come from the reduction in congestion on the existing modes of transport. A reduced number of trips on these existing modes will translate into less burning of fossil fuels, as well as fewer vehicular emissions. The reduction in fuel consumption (measured in unit vehicle operating costs for different vehicle categories on the road) is deemed to be the major contributor toward generating environmental benefits. Reduction in harmful emissions is also expected to contribute toward these environmental benefits. It is estimated that the metro system will reduce carbon monoxide emissions by 4,400 tons per annum and carbon dioxide emissions by 166,000 tons per annum.

Figure 29 captures the environmental benefits of Metro Lines 2A, 2B, and 7 (measured in terms of savings in volatile organic compounds as well as emissions) up to 2051.[21] These benefits are projected to be sustained into the future. Importantly, they are expected to increase strongly with each passing decade—i.e., the environmental benefits in 2041–2051 are estimated to be almost twice as much as the benefits in 2021–2031.

The benefits shown in Figure 29 are for only two metro lines in the Mumbai Metro Master Plan, which, as mentioned earlier, are projected to generate multifold benefits for the city upon accomplishment of the entire plan.

---

[21] ADB. 2019. *Report and Recommendation of the President to the Board of Directors: Proposed Loan to India for the Mumbai Metro Rail Systems Project*. Economic Analysis (accessible from the list of linked documents in Appendix 2). Manila.

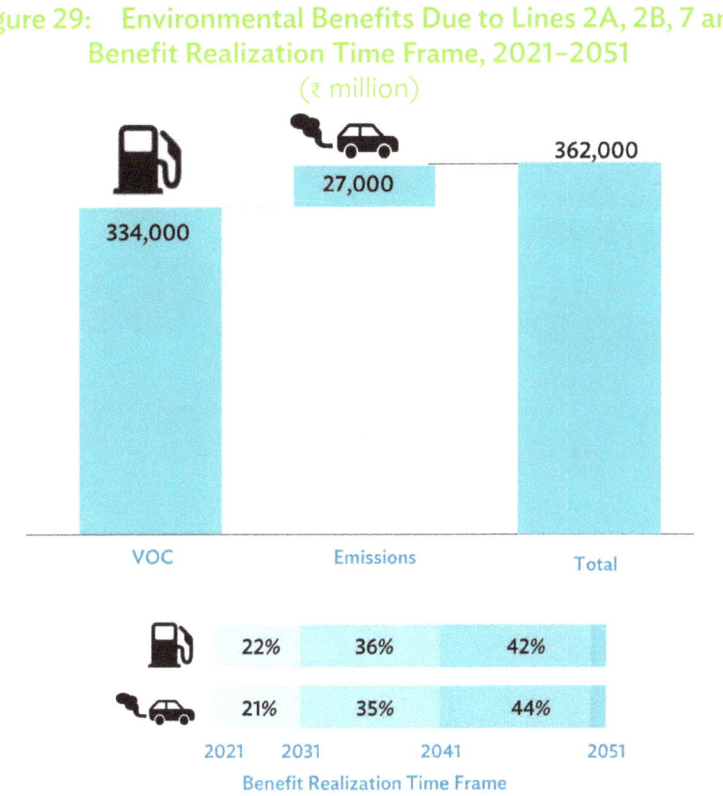

Figure 29: Environmental Benefits Due to Lines 2A, 2B, 7 and Benefit Realization Time Frame, 2021–2051
(₹ million)

₹ = Indian rupee, VOC = volatile organic compounds.
Source: Asian Development Bank. 2019. *Report and Recommendation of the President to the Board of Directors: Proposed Loan to India for the Mumbai Metro Rail Systems Project.* Economic Analysis (accessible from the list of linked documents in Appendix 2). Manila.

Private transport in Mumbai. The high number of cars in Mumbai is leading to further pressure on the city's limited road infrastructure, resulting in swelling traffic jam (photo by **Aleksandr Zykov** in *Flickr*).

Inside the metro trains. Metro trains provide a clean and comfortable mode of urban transport (photo by Placeontop in *Pixabay*).

Financial Sustainability

Financial Performance of Line 1

Public transport projects, such as the Mumbai Metro, are capital- and maintenance-intensive. The capital cost for such projects is typically funded by taxpayers' money, and some proportion comes from private players (in cases where the project has been considered on a public–private partnership basis). From the financiers' point of view, it becomes critical that the project is able to meet and exceed its investment objectives on a sustainable basis.

Currently, Line 1 is the only operational metro line in Mumbai. It is the first metro corridor in India to be constructed on public–private partnership basis. The Mumbai Metro One Private Limited (MMOPL) was formed wherein Reliance Infrastructure had a 69% stake, followed by a 26% stake of the Mumbai Metropolitan Region Development Authority (MMRDA) and a 5% stake of Veolia Transport (an international transport services company). Since the commencement of operations on Line 1 in 2014, the MMOPL has earned a cumulative revenue of ₹11.83 billion, while its cumulative operational expenditure has been ₹8.09 billion. As observed in Figure 30, the revenue of the MMOPL has grown at a compound annual growth rate of almost 18% since its inception.

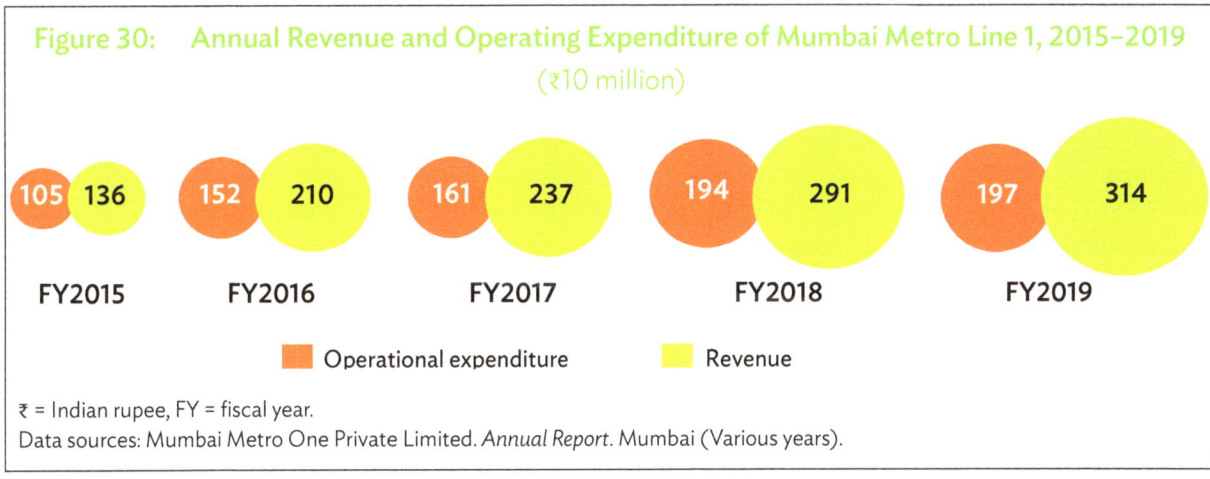

Figure 30: Annual Revenue and Operating Expenditure of Mumbai Metro Line 1, 2015–2019 (₹10 million)

₹ = Indian rupee, FY = fiscal year.
Data sources: Mumbai Metro One Private Limited. *Annual Report*. Mumbai (Various years).

Within the operational expenditure incurred by the MMOPL, manpower expenses account for the highest proportion, followed by repair and maintenance expenses (Figure 31).

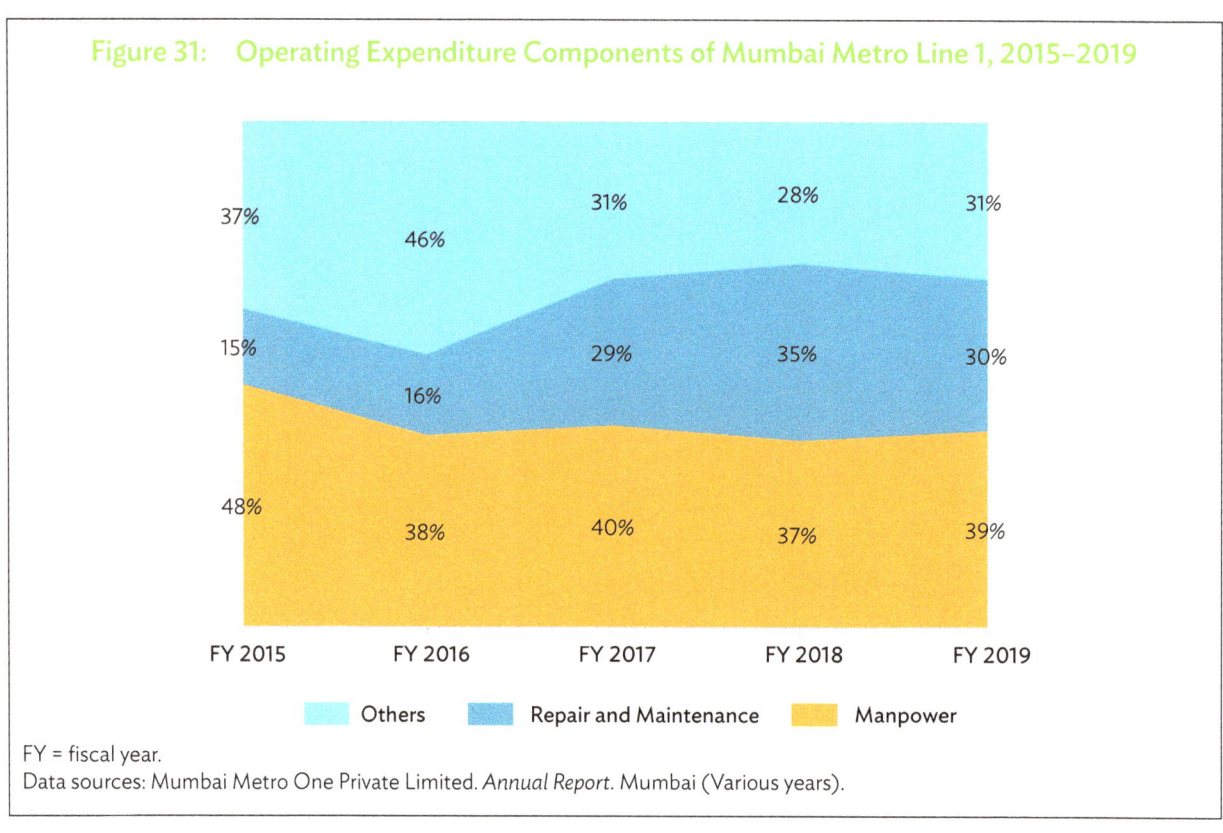

Figure 31: Operating Expenditure Components of Mumbai Metro Line 1, 2015–2019

FY = fiscal year.
Data sources: Mumbai Metro One Private Limited. *Annual Report*. Mumbai (Various years).

Financial Projections of Lines 2 and 7

Lines 2 and 7 are expected to be the next operational lines on the Mumbai Metro network. Their financial sustainability analysis, undertaken by the Asian Development Bank (ADB), factors in the capital costs, operating costs, and revenues to arrive at the financial feasibility of the lines (Figure 32). The capital costs include all costs financed by the MMRDA for civil construction (i.e., stations, tracks, and depots), rolling stock procurement, and supply and installation of signaling components. The operation and maintenance costs include staff, maintenance, overhead, and energy. The revenues are generated mainly from ticket sales and from non-farebox sources, such as advertising and leasing.

An important driver for the financial sustainability of the project will be fare-based revenues. Figure 33 compares the distance-wise fares of different modes of public transport in Mumbai with the proposed fares of Metro Lines 2 and 7. As illustrated, when compared over the average daily distance travelled by commuters on the Brihanmumbai Electricity Supply and Transport (BEST) buses (8.9 km), the proposed fares for Lines 2 and 7 of the Mumbai Metro are comparable with the BEST air-conditioned, as well as non-air-conditioned, buses. In terms of the average daily distance travelled by commuters on the Mumbai suburban trains (23.8 km), while the proposed fares for Metro Lines 2 and 7 are more than the fares for second-class suburban train travel, they are significantly lesser than the fares of first-class suburban train travel. Since the metro is expected to provide a journey that will be more comfortable, safer, and reliable than the air-conditioned BEST buses and first-class suburban train travel, the fare-based revenue is expected to grow under normal operating circumstances and help the financial sustainability of the project.

Financial Sustainability 55

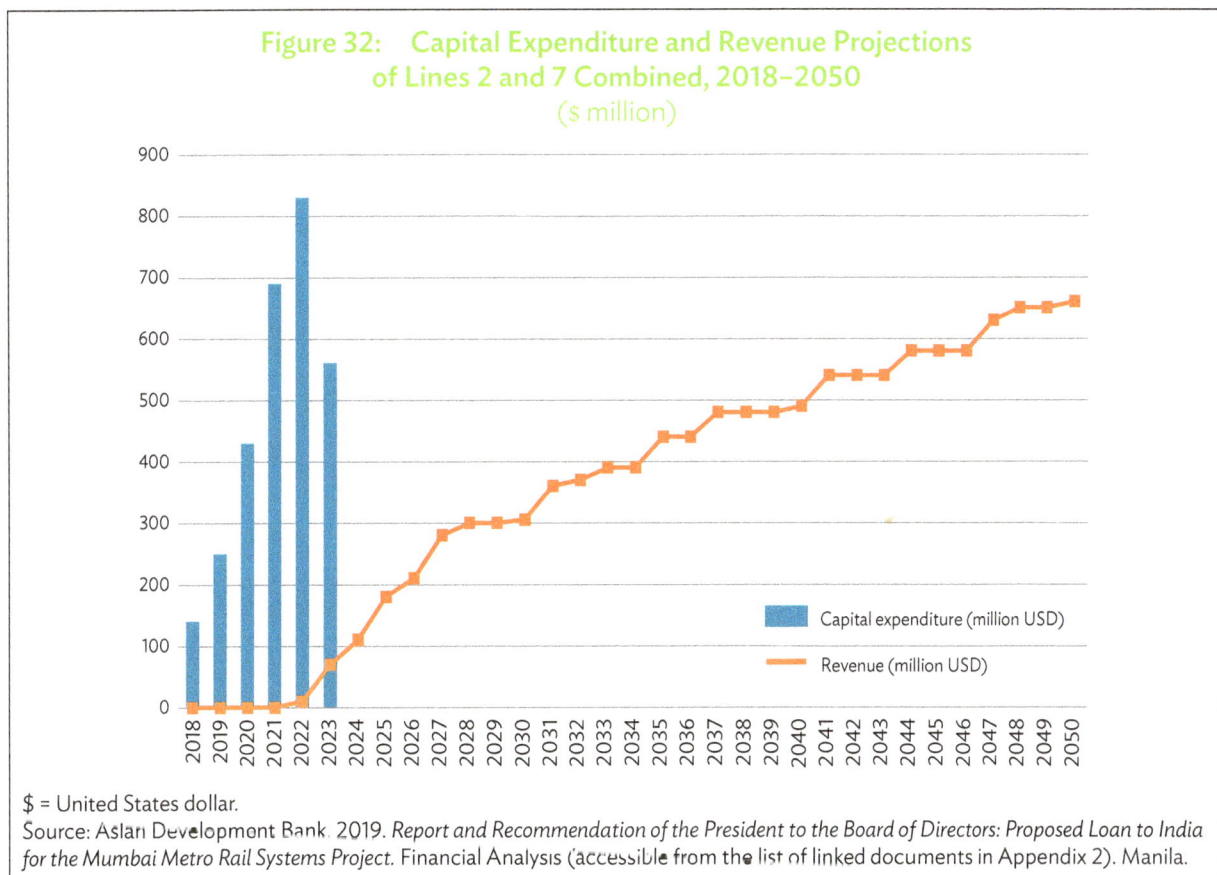

Figure 32: Capital Expenditure and Revenue Projections of Lines 2 and 7 Combined, 2018–2050
($ million)

$ = United States dollar.
Source: Asian Development Bank. 2019. *Report and Recommendation of the President to the Board of Directors: Proposed Loan to India for the Mumbai Metro Rail Systems Project*. Financial Analysis (accessible from the list of linked documents in Appendix 2). Manila.

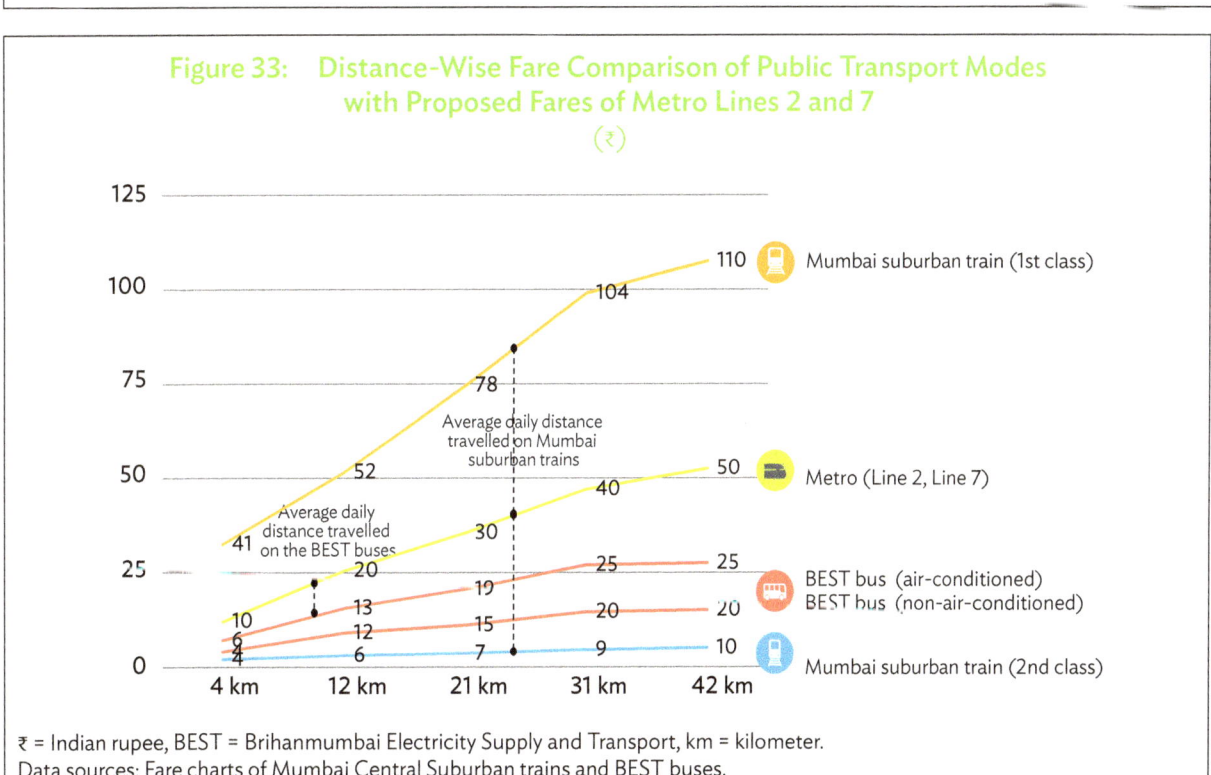

Figure 33: Distance-Wise Fare Comparison of Public Transport Modes with Proposed Fares of Metro Lines 2 and 7
(₹)

₹ = Indian rupee, BEST = Brihanmumbai Electricity Supply and Transport, km = kilometer.
Data sources: Fare charts of Mumbai Central Suburban trains and BEST buses.

Alternate Sources for Improving Financial Sustainability

Innovative sources are increasingly being considered to support capital-intensive transportation projects to improve their financial sustainability. Such sources help the authority hedge against uncertainty in the market projections as well as reduce the funding gap of the project.

Multiple urban transportation projects in India are already exploring these alternative sources of financing. For instance, the Government of Karnataka has recommended to raise ₹6.5 billion for the Bangalore Metro via sources like a metro levy and a levy on the additional floor area ratio (FAR). It has been prescribed that a metro levy of 5% of the value of the land shall be applied within the jurisdiction of the Bangalore Development Authority (BDA). Further, in the draft Master Plan for Bengaluru 2031, the BDA has proposed to increase the FAR up to 4.0 for properties lying within the 250-meter radius of the metro station. Charges of 10% for residential properties and 20% for commercial properties have also been proposed to be levied on the premium paid.[22] The funds accruing from this are to be credited to a Metro Infrastructure Fund, which will be managed by the BDA. It is likewise recommended that the Bangalore Metro Rail Corporation Limited will be entitled to up to 65% of these proceeds, and the rest will be shared between other related government institutions, such as the BDA and the Municipal Corporation. Similarly, the Government of Maharashtra has passed executive orders to increase the MMRDA's revenues, including (i) an increase in the stamp duty (from 5% to 6%) for property transactions, (ii) an increase in the development charge (from 4% to 6%) for new property, and (iii) a premium on additional floor space index (60% of the ready reckoner rate).

Specific to metro projects, the Government of Maharashtra has utilized an additional stamp duty and additional purchasable FAR for capturing land value for the Nagpur Metro project. The Government of Maharashtra amended the *Maharashtra Municipal Corporations Act 1949* and the *Maharashtra Region and Town Planning Act 1961* in 2017 to include the Nagpur Metro as a "Notified Vital Urban Transport Project." It implemented an additional 1% transaction value to the stamp duty upon the base rate of 5% in the jurisdiction of Nagpur. The full proceeds get credited to the Consolidated Fund of the State of Maharashtra and are used for financing the project. Further, it amended the Nagpur master plan to operationalize the transit-oriented development policy. This policy allowed a FAR of up to 4.0 along the 500-meter corridor on either side of the metro alignment, with 50% of the proceeds to be used for project financing. The Nagpur Metro has received ₹1.49 million from additional stamp duty (from 2017 to 2019), and proceeds from additional purchasable FAR for the same period reached ₹110 million (footnote 22). A key enabler in the Nagpur Metro case has been the appointment of the project special-purpose vehicle (Maha Metro) as the Special Planning Authority for designated areas along its alignment. Thus, the Maha Metro has been made responsible for granting development permissions and collecting the charges.

The MMRDA, being both the development authority as well as the developer and operator of the Mumbai Metro project, is exploring innovative sources for improving the sustainability of the project. The Government of Maharashtra increased the stamp duty from 5% to 6% in 2018. This would be applicable on all property transactions in Mumbai, and the proceeds would finance major transport infrastructure projects currently being undertaken by the Mumbai Metropolitan Region (MMR). However, in March 2020, the Government of Maharashtra announced a concession for 2 years in this stamp duty increase. This move is expected to boost the construction and realty sectors in Mumbai, which is especially needed during the coronavirus disease (COVID-19) pandemic times. Other value-capture financing instruments proposed by the MMRDA include the

---

[22] National Institute of Urban Affairs. 2020. *Land Value Capture for Transit Oriented Development: A Demonstration.* Knowledge Product 2. New Delhi.

increase in development charges by 100% and a transit-oriented development policy that allows for additional purchasable FAR on payment of a premium—50% of this premium is proposed to be dedicated toward financing of the metro.

It should be noted that the MMOPL is already implementing ideas, such as the station branding rights, as an alternative source of revenue. Station branding of Ghatkopar, Andheri, and Western Express Highway stations are a few successful examples. The MMOPL has also given retail space in its stations to several large retailers to generate additional revenue. This is being done in addition to revenue generated from activities such as train wrapping on Line 1.

Mass Transit Railway (MTR), Hong Kong, China. Passengers wait for the metro train to arrive at one of the MTR stations in Hong Kong, China (photo by Wilfredor in *Wikimedia Commons*).

Lessons from Other Metro Systems

Delhi Metro—Providing Equal Access to Everyone, Everywhere

Global metro systems provide strong evidence on how they have helped cities become safer, more equitable, and more sustainable. The metros considered for reference herein (starting with Delhi) are similar to Mumbai on parameters, such as socioeconomic environment, population density, pollution levels, real estate prices, etc.

Delhi is the national capital of India and is the center of the National Capital Region (NCR). It has experienced rapid growth over the last few decades and attracted people from all over the country. This increasing population placed excessive pressure on Delhi's existing public transportation infrastructure, which required upgrading. The Delhi Metro, which was the first in India, revolutionized public transportation in the country. Starting operations in 2002, it presently has a massive 389 km network with 285 stations, and is still expanding. The Delhi Metro's daily passenger journey, pre-COVID-19, is about 6 million; also, it provides accessibility to the people of surrounding areas, such as Noida, Gurugram, Ghaziabad, Faridabad, Ballabhgarh, and Bahadurgarh.

In a study to measure Delhi's economic and equity implications, it was found that its Gini coefficient decreased from 0.399 to 0.221 after the introduction of the metro.[23] This was possible because of the increased mobility and accessibility provided to the NCR citizens. The Delhi Metro has been successful in providing easy and equitable mobility to the NCR citizens and enabled them to access the major centers of education, health, and employment. This has helped people from all groups and communities to connect with the best available schools, hospitals, and industries. This equitable connectivity has, in turn, empowered the population to utilize the best available facilities.

A mapping of the Delhi Metro's network, shown in Figures 34, 35, and 36, highlights how it enables improved transport accessibility across all parts of the NCR, provides connectivity to these important centers of socioeconomic development and, thus, plays a key role in the uplift of the NCR. With improved access for everyone, the Delhi Metro is empowering the whole population. The Delhi Metro has put Delhi on the world map and has become a symbol of the city worldwide.

---

[23] K. Bhandari, H. Kato, and H. Yoshitsugu. 2009. Economic and Equity Evaluation of Delhi Metro. *International Journal of Urban Sciences*. 13 (2). pp. 187–203.

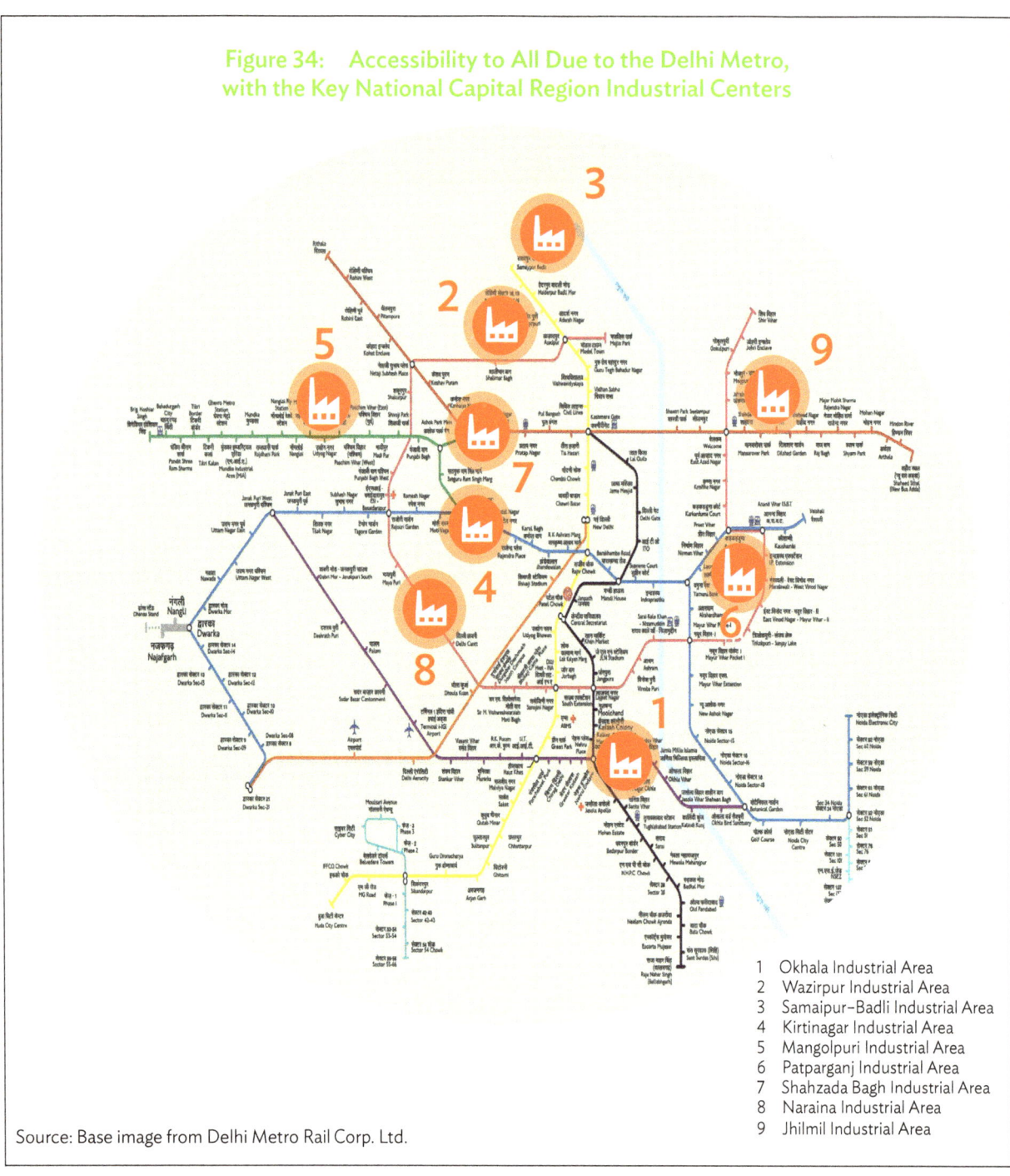

Figure 34: Accessibility to All Due to the Delhi Metro, with the Key National Capital Region Industrial Centers

1. Okhala Industrial Area
2. Wazirpur Industrial Area
3. Samaipur–Badli Industrial Area
4. Kirtinagar Industrial Area
5. Mangolpuri Industrial Area
6. Patparganj Industrial Area
7. Shahzada Bagh Industrial Area
8. Naraina Industrial Area
9. Jhilmil Industrial Area

Source: Base image from Delhi Metro Rail Corp. Ltd.

The construction and operationalization of the Mumbai Metro are expected to have similar impacts on the MMR. The direct connectivity and easy accessibility provided by the Mumbai Metro should enable the people to comfortably reach the centers of socioeconomic development (such as schools, hospitals, offices, etc.). This will, in turn, help the people in Mumbai improve key metrics such as literacy rate, employment rate, hospital accessibility, workforce participation (especially for women and the differently abled), among others. This will eventually reduce the income inequality and the Gini coefficient in Mumbai, as already witnessed in the case of Delhi.

Lessons from Other Metro Systems 61

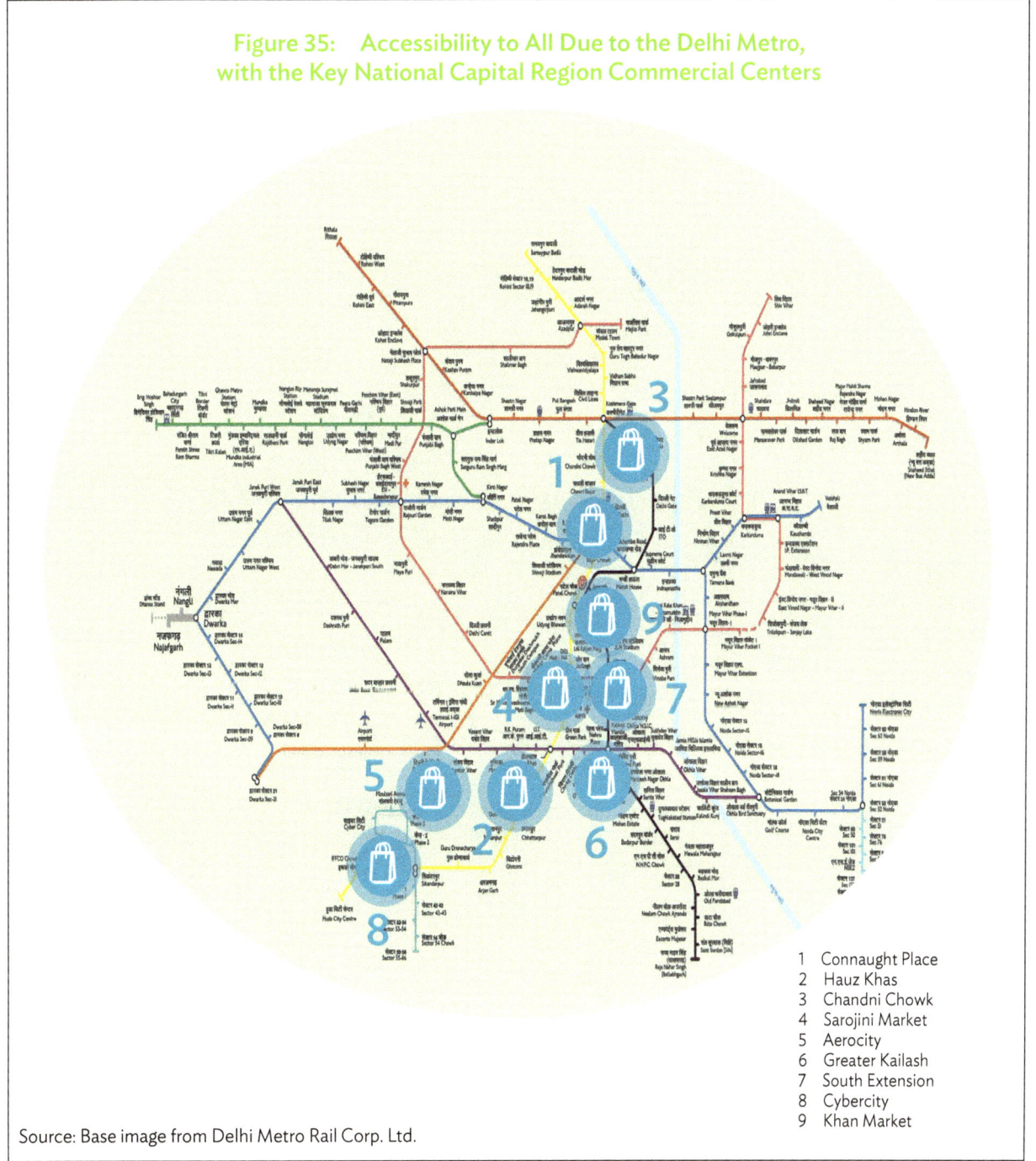

Figure 35: Accessibility to All Due to the Delhi Metro, with the Key National Capital Region Commercial Centers

1 Connaught Place
2 Hauz Khas
3 Chandni Chowk
4 Sarojini Market
5 Aerocity
6 Greater Kailash
7 South Extension
8 Cybercity
9 Khan Market

Source: Base image from Delhi Metro Rail Corp. Ltd.

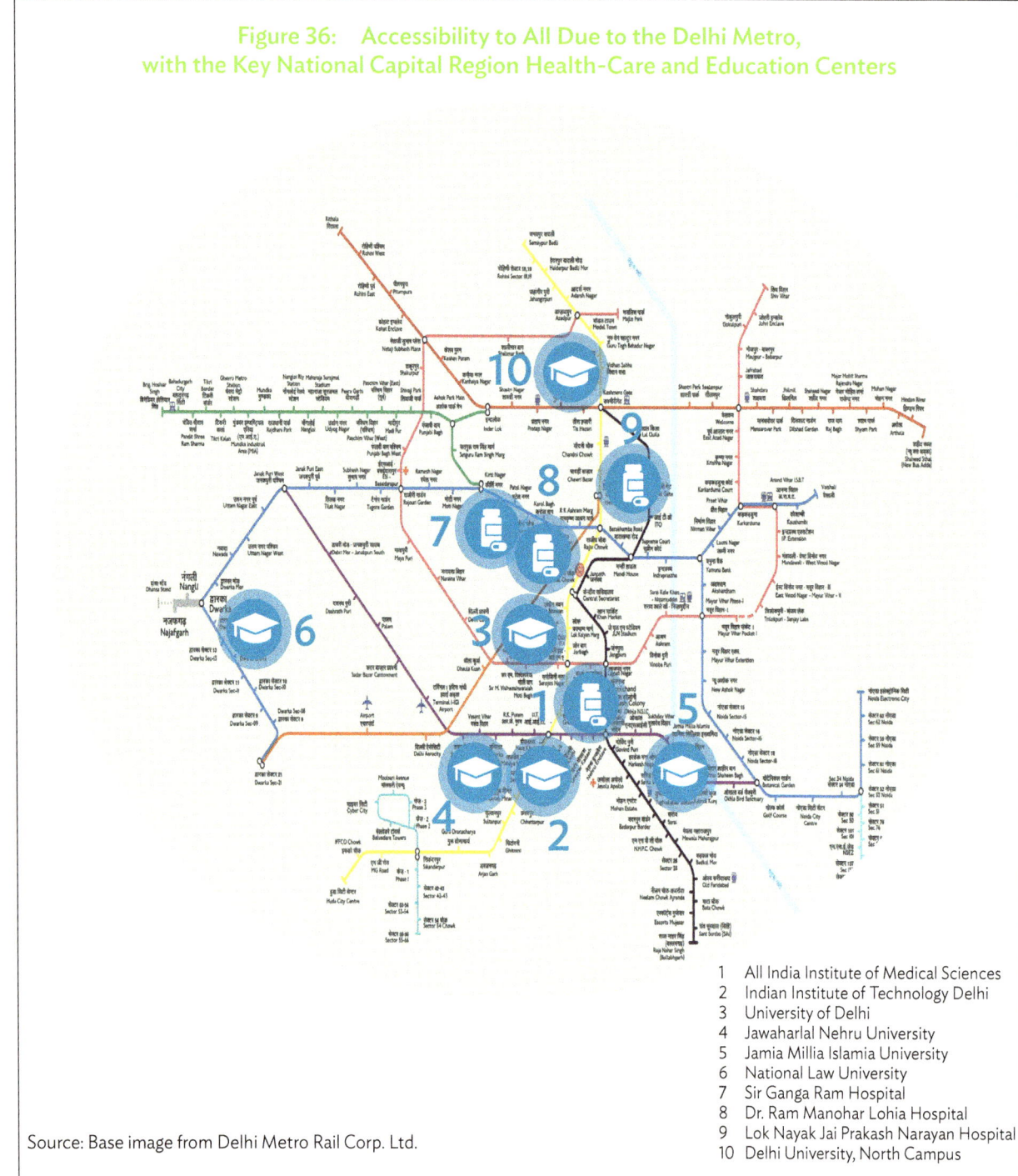

Figure 36: Accessibility to All Due to the Delhi Metro, with the Key National Capital Region Health-Care and Education Centers

Source: Base image from Delhi Metro Rail Corp. Ltd.

1 All India Institute of Medical Sciences
2 Indian Institute of Technology Delhi
3 University of Delhi
4 Jawaharlal Nehru University
5 Jamia Millia Islamia University
6 National Law University
7 Sir Ganga Ram Hospital
8 Dr. Ram Manohar Lohia Hospital
9 Lok Nayak Jai Prakash Narayan Hospital
10 Delhi University, North Campus

ns from Other Metro Systems

Manila Metro Rail Transit System—Providing a Transport Alternative in a Densely Populated and Highly Polluted City

Since the world has been battling the coronavirus disease (COVID-19) pandemic, there has been a sharp focus on personal health improvement and the role of governments to create systems that promote healthier lives. As COVID-19 severely impacts our respiratory systems, governments around the world (especially in developing countries) will have to turn their attention toward the growing hazard of air pollution. An improvement in the quality of air, as well as a reduction in the exposure to harmful air pollutants, may reduce the risk-exposure of the population. The metro rail transit in Manila, Philippines offers a healthier transportation option, as compared with other modes.

Manila is relevant for Mumbai because of similarities in their socioeconomic profiles, transport challenges, and geographical location (Figure 37).

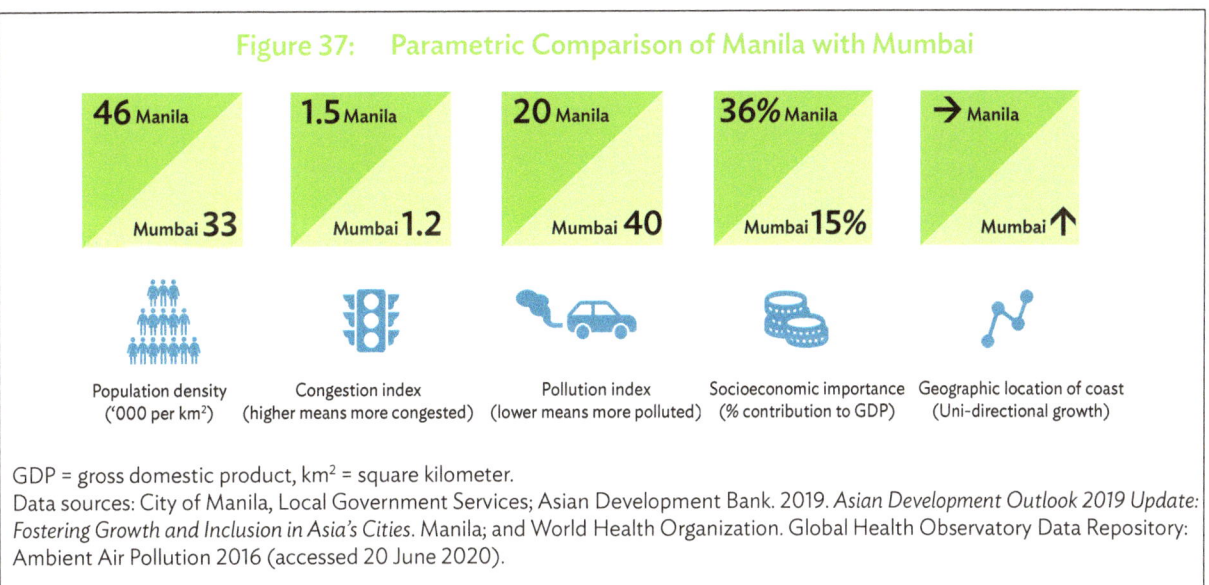

GDP = gross domestic product, km² = square kilometer.
Data sources: City of Manila, Local Government Services; Asian Development Bank. 2019. *Asian Development Outlook 2019 Update: Fostering Growth and Inclusion in Asia's Cities*. Manila; and World Health Organization. Global Health Observatory Data Repository: Ambient Air Pollution 2016 (accessed 20 June 2020).

Manila is one of the most crowded cities in the world and outranks Mumbai in terms of its population density, with 46,000 people per km², as compared with 33,000 per km² in Mumbai. Manila's existing, overutilized transport infrastructure is responsible for its high congestion index, compared with Mumbai. On average, it takes 50% more time to travel in peak hours compared with off-peak hours in Manila, while the equivalent number is at 20% for Mumbai.[24] Owing to the high population density and the transport congestion, Manila is ranked 20th in the most polluted cities in the world, while Mumbai is ranked 40th (footnote 18). Manila contributes strongly to the country's economic output, much like Mumbai. In terms of geographic location, Manila is located on the coastline, just like Mumbai. This limits the ability of the city to spatially expand, and the consequent unidirectional growth puts excessive pressure on the existing infrastructure.

---

[24] ADB. 2019. *Asian Development Outlook 2019 Update: Fostering Growth and Inclusion in Asia's Cities*. Manila.

As captured in the research paper, "An Analysis of Metro Manila MRT-3 (2016)," the Manila Metro Rail Transit Line 3 (MRT-3) has benefited the population by reducing exposure to harmful $PM_{2.5}$ particles. A comparison of exposure to $PM_{2.5}$ particles when passengers are travelling via buses or jeepneys (which are the main mode of transport in Manila) with exposure when travelling via the metro line reveals the stark difference between these modes. Intermodal comparison between the $PM_{2.5}$ exposure while travelling via the MRT-3 system and bus has been plotted in Figure 38. As observed, people travelling via buses in Manila were, on average, exposed to more than 1.5 times $PM_{2.5}$ emissions (60 µg/m³) as compared with the MRT-3 system (38 µg/m³). The highest exposure to $PM_{2.5}$ of people travelling via buses was found to be at 125 µg/m³, while those travelling via the metro line had approximately 25% lesser exposure at 90 µg/m³. Further, almost 65% of the passengers travelling via buses were exposed to $PM_{2.5}$ emissions that were in a broad and higher range of 20–100 µg/m³, while 65% of the passengers travelling via the metro line were exposed to $PM_{2.5}$ emissions that were in a narrow and lower range of 28-55 µg/m³.[25] This data analysis indicates the relative health benefit for passengers who choose to travel via the metro systems in densely populated and highly polluted cities like Manila.

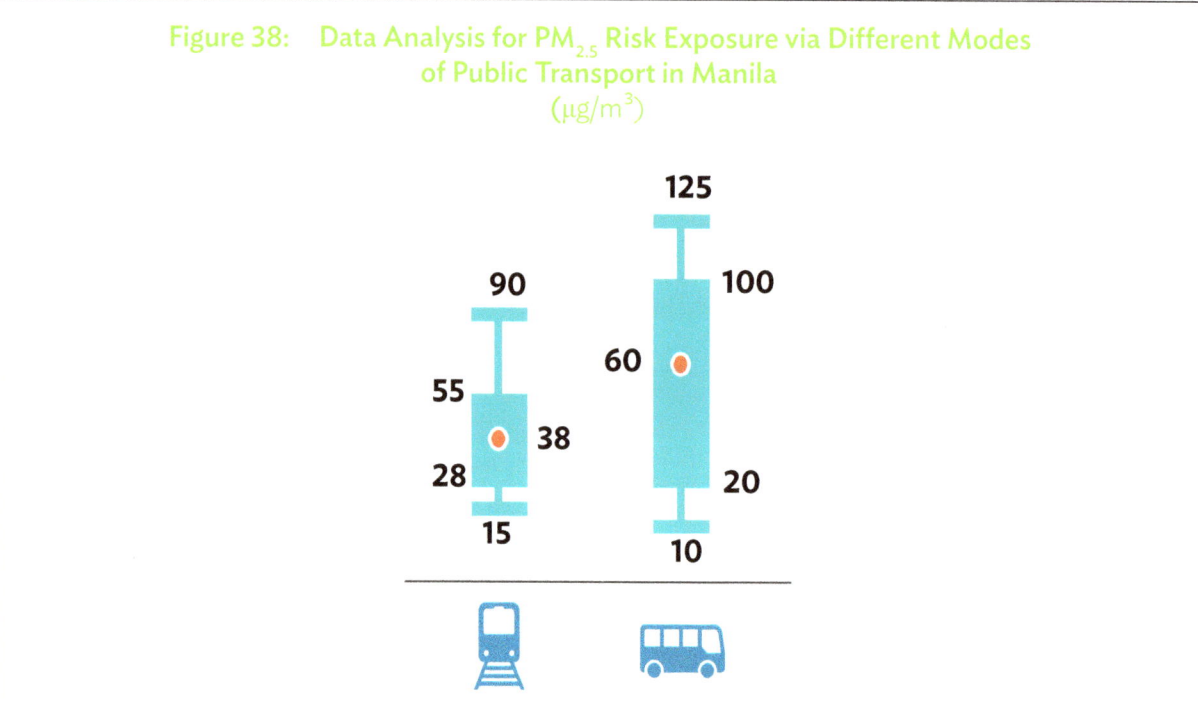

Figure 38: Data Analysis for $PM_{2.5}$ Risk Exposure via Different Modes of Public Transport in Manila
(µg/m³)

µg/m³ = microgram per cubic meter, $PM_{2.5}$ = particulate matter with less than 2.5 micrometers in diameter.
Data source: A. Mijares, M. Suzuki, and T. Yai. 2016. Passenger Satisfaction and Mental Adaptation under Adverse Conditions: Case Study in Manila. *Journal of Public Transportation*. 19 (4). pp. 144–160.

Thus, travelling via the metro, as compared with conventional road-based public transport systems, reduces the risk exposure of people to harmful $PM_{2.5}$ particles. This fact becomes even more critical in the COVID-19 period and points to the long-term environmental and health benefits of using metro rail transit systems over other modes of transport. Stronger patronage of the Mumbai Metro is, thus, expected to contribute toward healthier lungs for the people of Mumbai.

---

[25] A. Mijares, M. Suzuki, and T. Yai. 2016. Passenger Satisfaction and Mental Adaptation under Adverse Conditions: Case Study in Manila. *Journal of Public Transportation*. 19 (4). pp. 144–160.

Rail + Property Model—Providing Financial Sustainability for Hong Kong, China Metro

Hong Kong, China is one of the most densely populated cities in Asia, with more than 6,000 people per km^2. It is one of Asia's biggest financial centers, and its public transportation system caters to more than 11 million passenger journeys daily. The most important mode of public transport in Hong Kong, China is the Mass Transit Railway (MTR), which is constructed and operated by the Mass Transit Railway Corporation (MTRC). The MTRC was established in 1975 and currently has a network of more than 220 km and 90 stations.

The MTRC is globally renowned for its exceptional operational and financial performance. In 2019, it reported a near-perfect adherence to time-tabled operations (99.9% on-time passenger journeys) and carried more than 1.9 billion passengers. Further, while most metro systems in the world rely on public financial support, the MTRC operates without government subsidy. Yet, it still manages to be profitable, primarily because of the revenues it makes from its real estate business.

Not only has the MTR's revenue seen a strong year-on-year annual growth of almost 7% in 2010–2019, but it has also seen a strong and continuous contribution from its real estate business, which contributed 48% to the MTR's overall revenue of HK$54.5 billion in 2019 (Figure 39). The MTR generated an overall profit of HK$10 billion during this time.[26]

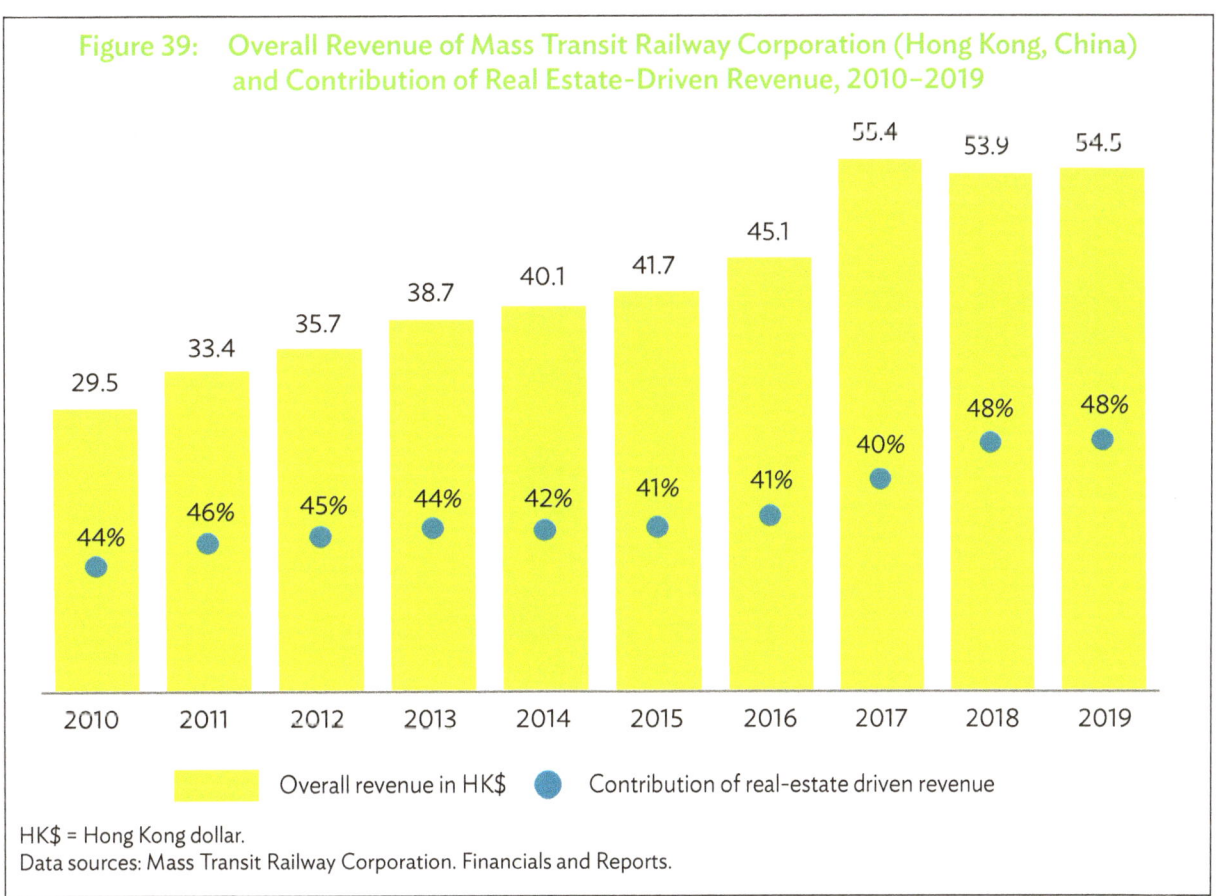

Figure 39: Overall Revenue of Mass Transit Railway Corporation (Hong Kong, China) and Contribution of Real Estate-Driven Revenue, 2010–2019

HK$ = Hong Kong dollar.
Data sources: Mass Transit Railway Corporation. Financials and Reports.

[26] Mass Transit Railway Corporation. Financials and Reports.

The real estate business of the MTR is centered around capturing the increased value of land due to the construction and operation of its metro lines. Land value capture follows the rationale that increased accessibility to an efficient transport system adds value to the real estate in its vicinity. Research indicates that land premiums in Hong Kong, China are in the range of 5%-17% for housing units in proximity to railways (which can further increase if the design incorporates transit-oriented structures, such as footbridges and skywalks, for seamless connectivity). Since this value increase is derived from public investments, the public authorities should capture the increment in the land and/or real estate value, which can then be used to repay part of the costs associated with the transport infrastructure.

Thus, the MTRC has adopted a "Rail + Property" model that enables it to capture the increase in land value as a result of the constructed transport infrastructure. This model has empowered the MTRC to become financially self-reliant.

At the project planning stage itself, the MTRC prepares the master plan and identifies property development sites along the railway. It obtains all necessary approvals and purchases the development rights (for a period of 50 years) from the government to develop the properties above the railway stations, depots, and on the land adjacent to the railway. These development rights are purchased at a land premium paid to the government known as the "before rail" land premium, which does not factor in the expected increase in value resulting from the transport connectivity. The MTRC then undertakes the tendering process to allocate these property development rights to private developers on the "after rail" increased land premium. The private developers bear the costs and risks associated with the construction and commercialization of the residential and commercial properties and enter into profit-sharing agreements with the MTRC (Figure 40).

The above arrangements between the key stakeholders highlight how the MTRC manages to capture the differential in the "before rail" and "after rail" premiums that forms the basis of the Rail + Property model and enables the MTRC to become financially sustainable. It is important to note that the MTRC is responsible for master planning and designing, obtaining and facilitating approvals related to real estate development, tendering

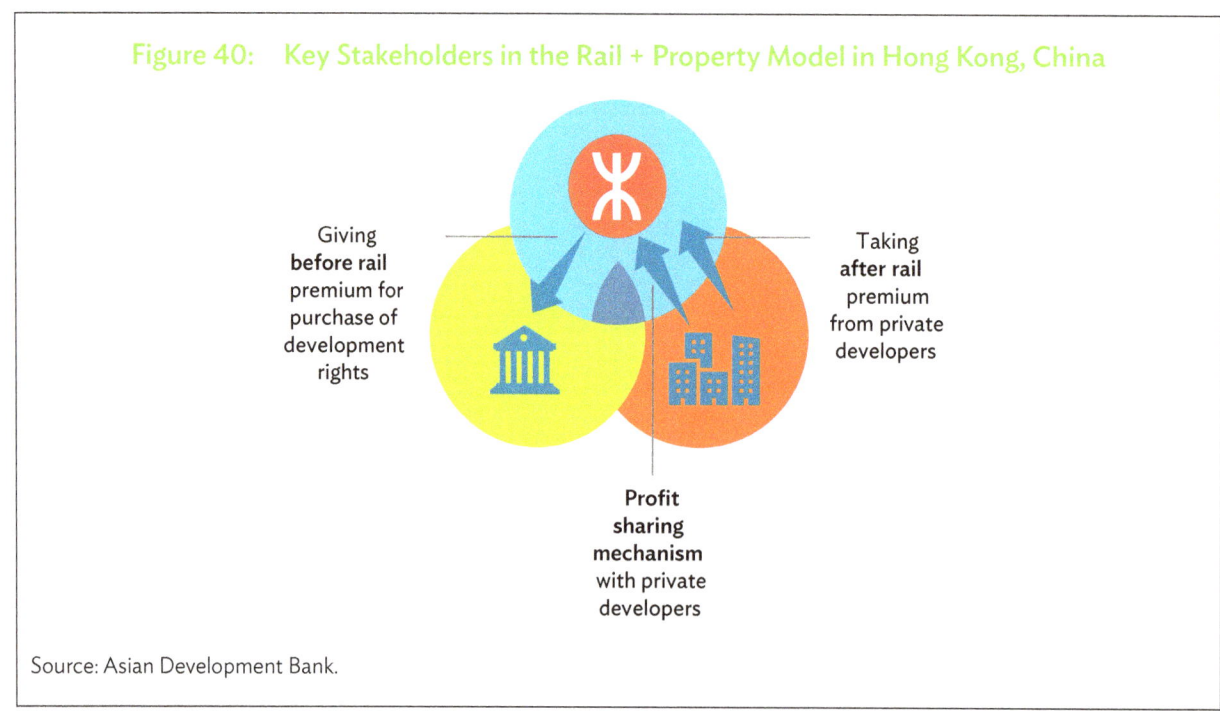

Figure 40: Key Stakeholders in the Rail + Property Model in Hong Kong, China

Source: Asian Development Bank.

land parcel development rights to private developers, liaising between the government and private developers, and monitoring the real estate development. The private developers are responsible for all construction risks and associated costs; all commercialization risks and associated costs; and enabling expenses related to sales, marketing, financing, etc. The government is only involved in selling the land development rights to the MTRC and providing all necessary approvals.

Figure 41 summarizes the key factors that have made the Rail + Property model successful for the MTRC. One of the model's biggest success factors is the scarcity of land in Hong Kong, China. Since private developers have limited options for developing properties, they are attracted to developing properties above railway stations, despite the extra costs and efforts involved. Further, since the real estate prices in Hong Kong, China have been skyrocketing over the last 4 decades (house prices have grown 15 times since 1980), private developers have optimistic expectations from the property market and are keen to participate in the Rail + Property model.[27] Another important success factor is the high volume of traffic (11 million daily passenger journeys) that creates a huge commercial potential for properties connected to the railway. Finally, the close relationship between the MTRC and the government also plays a critical role in making this model successful. As the government is the majority shareholder in the MTRC with 77% ownership, it benefits indirectly from the profits made by the MTRC. The Rail + Property model also aligns with the government's intention to drive growth at the local level.

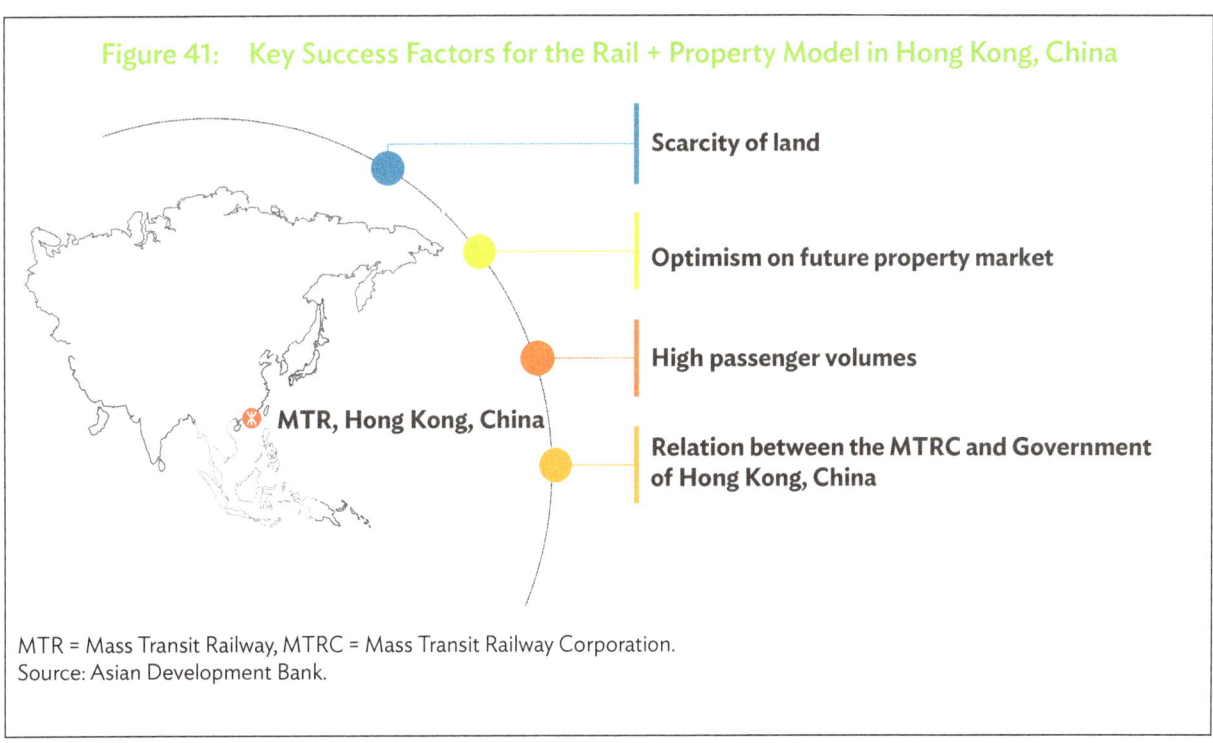

Figure 41: Key Success Factors for the Rail + Property Model in Hong Kong, China

- Scarcity of land
- Optimism on future property market
- High passenger volumes
- Relation between the MTRC and Government of Hong Kong, China

MTR = Mass Transit Railway, MTRC = Mass Transit Railway Corporation.
Source: Asian Development Bank.

---

[27] M. Verougstraete and H. Zeng. 2014. *Land Value Capture Mechanism: The Case of the Hong Kong Mass Transit Railway*. Public–private partnerships case study prepared for the United Nations Economic and Social Commission for Asia and the Pacific. July.

Inside a metro train. As metro operations gradually restart, passengers can be seen wearing masks inside the metro trains (photo by Richard Atrero de Guzman/Asian Development Bank).

Public Transportation in the COVID-19 Era

Behavioral Shifts and Patterns Expected Due to COVID-19

The coronavirus disease (COVID-19) is one of the most severe public health and economic crises that the modern-day world has faced. It will have lingering medium- and long-term impacts on businesses and lifestyles. With several national and regional borders being closed to contain the spread of the virus, public transport systems have been severely hit. The journey back to a normal operating environment will be long and uphill. The lockdowns imposed in several countries, states, and cities across the world have been implemented to reduce the risk of virus transmission. However, this has resulted in significant losses on the public transport networks. Metro operators in India, as well as across the world, are facing heavy losses and several challenges because of COVID-19.

Some of the major challenges being faced by mass transit systems include low fare-related revenues; higher operating expenses as a result of additional measures undertaken to enhance passenger safety; and uncertainty in the short-, medium-, and long-term financial and operational planning.

A survey conducted by the Cities Forum et al. (2020) on the expected impact of COVID-19 on cities and mobility highlights some expected future trends.[28] The survey covered the points of view of more than 550 urban mobility practitioners and experts from more than 45 countries. As shown in Figure 42, 89% of respondents consider work-from-home arrangement to become an acceptable norm in businesses. This is expected to reduce the demand for office buildings, decrease the sizes of offices, and reduce the overall demand for commercial real estate (specifically outside the inner city). All these factors will impact the demand for mobility as more people will be able to opt for working from home rather than commuting daily to work. Approximately 47% of respondents believe that the overall demand for mobility (covering all modes of transport) will at least remain subdued till 2022. However, the respondents have expressed strong confidence in public health interventions as an enabler to drive people back to public modes of transport, with 92% expecting that measures like enforced social distancing, penalties for noncompliance of face mask protocol, and proactive public health messaging can drive people back to the public modes of transport.

---

[28] Cities Forum et al. 2020. *Impact of COVID-19 on Cities and Mobility*. White Paper on Global Cities and Mobility Survey. A Project Impact report. June.

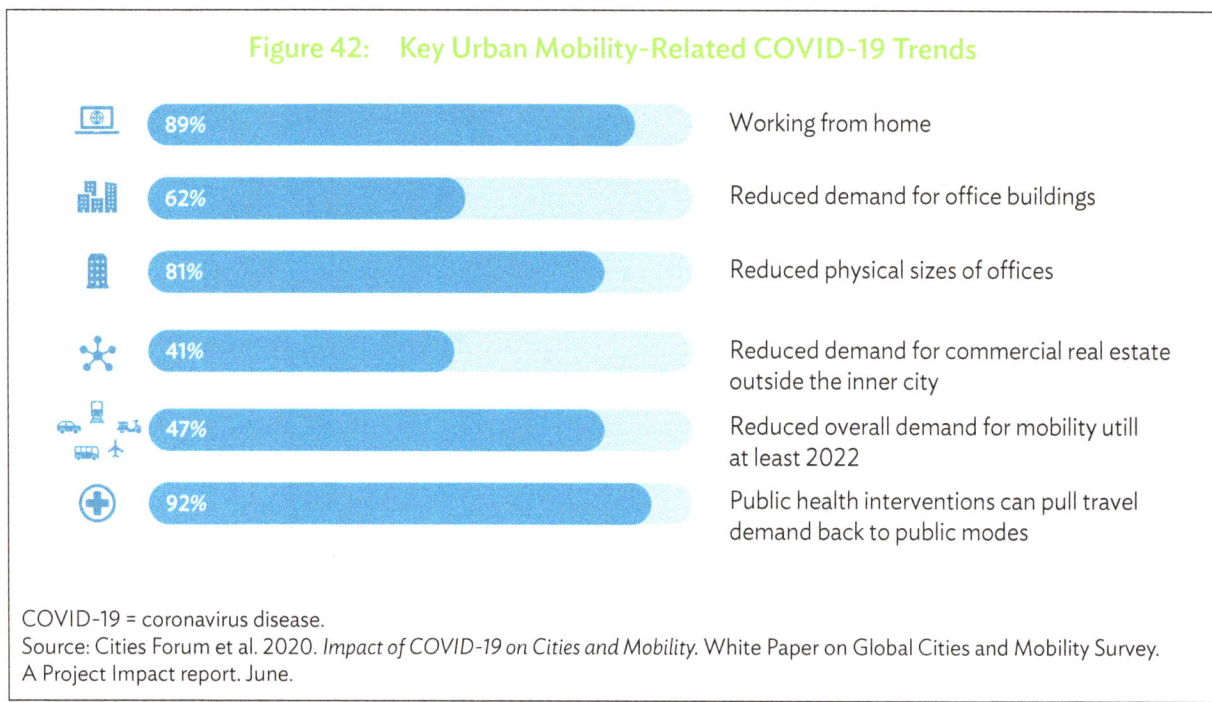

Figure 42: Key Urban Mobility-Related COVID-19 Trends

- 89% Working from home
- 62% Reduced demand for office buildings
- 81% Reduced physical sizes of offices
- 41% Reduced demand for commercial real estate outside the inner city
- 47% Reduced overall demand for mobility utill at least 2022
- 92% Public health interventions can pull travel demand back to public modes

COVID-19 = coronavirus disease.
Source: Cities Forum et al. 2020. *Impact of COVID-19 on Cities and Mobility.* White Paper on Global Cities and Mobility Survey. A Project Impact report. June.

Importantly, delay in the development of a vaccine will increase the hesitance of people to venture into public spaces, and this is likely to sustain the reduced demand for public transportation. Such aspects are expected to reduce passenger ridership in the medium to long term, if sufficient interventions are not taken. Countries around the world are exploring options for gradually and safely relaxing the lockdown conditions; thus, a calibrated reopening of the public transport networks is also foreseen. The metro systems have already started exploring ways to mitigate the impact of the above risks and challenges. Measures are being planned (or already implemented) to improve the financial and operational conditions of the metro systems, as well as enhance the safety and health of the commuters.

Some commuter-oriented measures being adopted globally include the 100% monitoring and screening of passengers using thermometers, advanced image recognition algorithms to capture non-adherence to the wearing of face mask protocol, installation of mobile applications for health monitoring, regular sanitization of stations and coaches, innovative passenger entrance mechanisms to avoid passenger queueing, installation of hand sanitizers, mandatory usage of masks, social distancing norms inside stations and coaches, and compulsory use of digital payments and smartcards.

Taipei,China's metro rail transit system agency has installed infrared cameras to measure the body temperature of passengers before allowing them entry into the metro stations. This enables the agency to monitor and prevent passengers with temperatures above 38 degrees Celsius from boarding the train. A vast majority of metros in the Republic of Korea, London, and New York, as well as in India, have already started regular intensive sanitization of the trains and the metro stations. The metro agencies in Beijing and Germany are exploring data analytics-based options for passenger density management at the stations. Data drawn from various sensor technologies and security cameras (along with advanced machine learning and intelligent automation tools) help to understand and track movements of passengers in and out of stations, determine average waiting times, identify areas with high crowd density (such as concourses, stairwells, platforms), etc. When the crowd threshold limits in certain areas are reached, alarms are triggered, which guide actions to be taken, such as redirecting passenger flows or temporarily closing certain areas. Further, the operators can also improve their sanitation responsiveness and guide teams to areas that need the most cleaning, based on the crowd density handled. The development and adoption of mobile phone apps for passengers' safety and self-checking are also expected to increase passenger confidence. Such apps are providing inputs to authorities needed in deciding whether to allow or disallow access to people, based on those they have interacted with in the recent past, while also giving confidence to people about those allowed to enter the facilities.

Business-oriented measures, such as identifying ways to reduce the operating expenses, rationalizing routes, planning for maximizing non-fare revenues, revising timetables, giving high priority to transit-oriented development, and focusing on freight services, are helping set up barriers to safeguard owners and operating organizations.

In the long term, a gradual shift away from public transport modes is not a sustainable solution as it will lead to a further increase in the number of private vehicles on the roads. This will have multiple negative impacts including increased harmful emissions and limiting transport connectivity options for the low-income population, women, and the differently abled. Strategic interventions from the respective governments, such as changes in relevant policies and financial support, are expected to support the sector in the long term.

The time-bound construction of the Mumbai Metro (especially Lines 2, 3, and 7, which are estimated to be operational by 2021) is expected to help the city. Currently, more than 40% of commuter journeys in Mumbai happen in densely overcrowded (almost 14 passengers per square meter) suburban trains. The additional transport capacity created by Lines 2, 3, and 7 and other planned metro lines in Mumbai will facilitate in reducing the congestion levels in the suburban trains, where currently social distancing norms are extremely difficult to achieve.

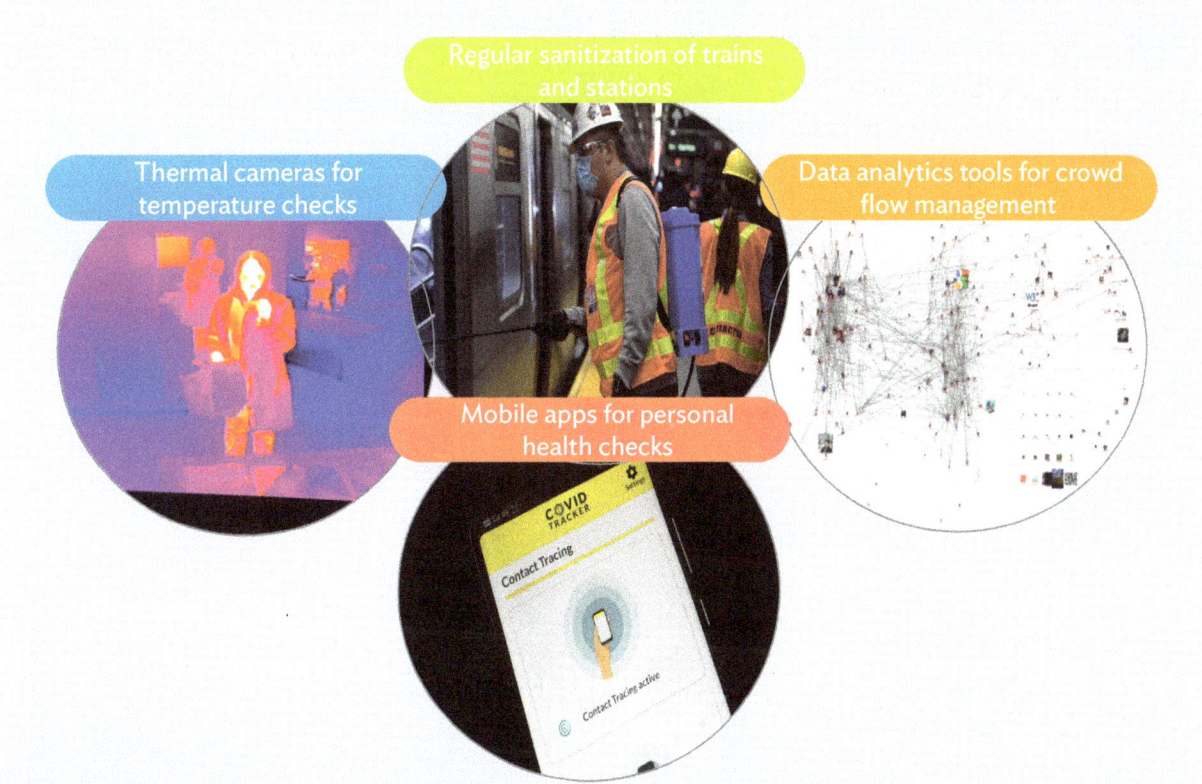

Health and safety protocols in the Metro. Global Metro organizations have been adopting several COVID-19-focused safety interventions (images are illustrative taken from photos by H. Cowper in *Flickr*, M. A. Hermann in *Wikimedia Commons*, M. Smith in *Flickr*, and M. Verch in *Flickr*).

Traffic along a street in Mumbai. Vehicles plying the busy streets of Mumbai include auto-rickshaws, buses, private cars, taxis, and two-wheelers (photo by Neeraj Pattath in *Wikimedia Commons*).

Conclusion

A New Era for Public Transportation in Mumbai

The realization of the Mumbai Metro Master Plan can herald a new era for public transportation in Mumbai. The completion of all 12 lines will provide easy access to everyone across Mumbai. The metro will not only reduce pressure on the existing suburban railway and buses, but also provide enhanced safety. It will create a modern transport system for the growth of India's financial capital, while also providing the much-needed East–West connectivity.

The Mumbai Metro is projected to drive a modal shift while also improving the travel conditions for all commuters. It will provide a modern and high-quality transport option for people in the low-income groups, women, and the differently abled through an air-conditioned, noise-free, dust-free, and comfortable mode of transport. It will connect many pockets in Mumbai that are currently not connected.

The Mumbai Metro will improve transport accessibility for everyone to the important centers of socioeconomic development, such as schools, hospitals, and business centers. It is also anticipated to reduce the number of private vehicles in use and thus reduce carbon dioxide emissions, as well as the associated environmental, business, and social costs of traffic congestion. This, in turn, is expected to improve the air quality in Mumbai. The metro lines are further expected to provide improved safety to the people of Mumbai as the metro tracks will be elevated and not constructed at the ground level. For example, residents living alongside the tracks will have reduced risk exposure to passing trains. The elevated tracks will also eliminate the risk of trespassing as well as flooding, which is a recurring problem for suburban trains in Mumbai, especially in the monsoon season.

By its design, the Mumbai Metro commuters will not be able to cross the metro lines between platforms nor can they be accidentally pushed onto the lines due to the platform screen doors that will open only when the train has arrived at the platform. Overall, the Mumbai Metro will help improve the quality of life of the people in Mumbai. Overall, the Mumbai Metro will help improve the quality of life of the people in Mumbai.

"Changing buses and literally chasing after autos to get to school has been a problem I've had to face for the last two years. But now with the metro taking me from my house at Marol to school in Andheri West, travelling has been largely a trouble-free affair."

"From my house at Versova, every day I had to spend 120 rupees and waste an hour to get to JB Nagar. Now I reach in 10 minutes by metro."

"I would call the metro a huge blessing as it is super fast, convenient and a great means of travel for me from home to work and back."

Commuting via the Mumbai Metro. Happy Mumbaikar commuters shared their testimonials on how the Metro has changed their lives (images are illustrative taken from photos by Bernard Gagnon in *Wikimedia Commons*, PlaneMad in *Wikimedia Commons*, and Nooranadu mohan in *Wikimedia Commons*).

The metro system in Mumbai can strongly contribute toward developing a modern and safe rail-based urban transit system that can reduce pollution, reduce traffic congestion, increase the modal share of public transport, and improve the overall quality of the city's transport system.

The Mumbai Metro can truly make the city more equitable, safer, and cleaner.

Commuters waiting for a metro train in India. Metros have become the lifeline of cities in India (photo from Shady59 in *Wikimedia Commons*).

Mumbai Metropolitan Region Development Authority (MMRDA). The MMRDA staff are all smiles as they shoot their "Mumbai in Minutes" campaign video (photo by MMRDA).

www.ingramcontent.com/pod-product-compliance
Lightning Source LLC
Chambersburg PA
CBHW061139230426
43662CB00026B/2473